TRUE STORY

TRUE STORY

On the Life and Death of My Brother

HELEN HUMPHREYS

A complete catalogue record for this book can be obtained
from the British Library on request

First published as *Nocturne* in 2013 by
HarperCollins Publishers Limited, Toronto

First published as *True Story* in 2013 by Serpent's Tail,
an imprint of Profile Books Ltd
3A Exmouth House
Pine Street
London EC1R 0JH
www.serpentstail.com

ISBN 978 1 84668 914 7
eISBN 978 1 84765 889 0

Printed and bound by CPI Group (UK) Ltd, Croydon CRO 4 YY

10 9 8 7 6 5 4 3 2 1

MIX
Paper from
responsible sources
FSC® C020471

I

TACET

II

TACET

III

TACET

−1961 score of *4'33"* by John Cage

For my sister

This is what happened after you died.

We took the plastic bag with your clothes, and the plastic bag with your pills. The bag with the pills weighed more.

Outside, the sky was red over the mountains and the air was cold as we walked through the parking lot. It was 5:30 in the afternoon of December third. You had died at 4:20, in room 351 of the Burnaby General Hospital in Vancouver.

You looked more like yourself with the tubes in you than when we unhooked you from the ventilator. At the moment of your death you left us so quickly that it was almost the most shocking thing.

On the wall of the nurses' station were the ICU

rules of conduct. The number one rule was to always offer the patient's family some hope. You would have laughed at that, if you had been alive.

Later, when you came to me in the dream, you were wearing your old jean jacket, which meant that we were teenagers, still living in our parents' house. You said that it was hard work to be dead, and you asked me to tell you what had happened since you died.

So I write this down for you.

1

The dog lies on the rug making suckling noises while she sleeps. She's still a puppy, still bouncy with energy one moment, then flopped over with exhaustion the next. Hazel, the dog you knew, is dead. In an awful confluence of events, she died the same week that you did, Martin, although her death was an easier one than yours. The vet came to the house. Before that the dog ate a piece of steak and a whole chocolate bar. Before that I took her for a drive past all the places where we had once lived together, and the green spaces where she liked to run.

I probably got the new Vizsla too soon after the old one, but her need of me has turned out to be a good thing.

It's late at night. The house is quiet, and the world outside is quiet too. The sun set earlier behind a grey bank of clouds that promised rain all day and never delivered.

On a clear evening, I can see the sunset from the dining-room window, which faces west. I have a new house from the one you remember—a white row house on the other side of town. It has large, spacious rooms and when I first moved in last summer I brought no furniture with me, just a mattress that I put on the bedroom floor, and a couch for the living room. I ate standing up at the counter in the kitchen, or sitting on the couch and balancing a plate on my knees. It was a relief to have nothing in the house. I liked the echo of the empty rooms. I liked not being surrounded by my possessions and the memories attached to them.

It's late, Martin, but if you were alive, you would be awake too and I could call you up now and we would talk into the night. I would tell you that the old guys next door put six solar-powered lanterns on the path up to our houses, making the approach look a bit like a runway, only now two of the lanterns (the ones on my side of the path) don't work, but I haven't the heart to remove them.

I would tell you that the people on the other side

of me have moved out, and how I woke one night when they were still living there to hear the man calling out, repeatedly, "Oh Lord, Jesus Christ," and I thought they were having a religious revival meeting at three in the morning, until I came to my senses and realized they were just having sex.

You would like that story, although you might not be listening to me, might be distracted and making a kind of humming noise that was supposed to mean you were listening when I knew, in fact, that you weren't. I would have to say, "You're not listening to me," and you would say, *What?* and then we would both laugh.

2

You're buried here, in this town, Kingston, a place you never lived. But it seemed better to put you where our sister and I could look after your grave than to have you buried where you chose to live, three thousand miles away on the West Coast. I'm pretty sure you wouldn't approve of this decision, but it seemed important. Cathy goes out to the cemetery most weeks and cleans your stone, which is black and shiny, like the grand piano you used to play. We put the first two bars of one of your last compositions on the stone and your name, *Martin James Humphreys,* and the dates, *May 20, 1964–December 3, 2009,* that bracketed your short life, and the single word *Pianist* underneath that.

You're buried in a plain pine box, and because we didn't want you embalmed, your body is in a steel liner inside that box so that you could be flown east on the plane. The steel liner made your coffin very heavy, and on the day of your funeral we staggered under the weight of it as we carried it from the hearse to the graveside. The day you were buried was cold and windy, so bitterly cold that the whole affair seemed like a scene from a Russian novel. I accidentally locked Dad in the car when we got to the cemetery. He banged feebly on the windshield and it took a while before someone heard his muffled yelling and came to tell me. We lurched over the snowy ground with your coffin and the wind filled out the vestments of the minister so that she looked like a chess piece as she said the words over your body. Mum had taken a photo of your dead body as you were put into the steel liner at the funeral parlour in B.C. I don't know why she did this, and I have refused to look at the photo. I watched you die and I don't want to see you dead, to be reminded that you are dead, but I can't say that I'll never look at that photo, because one of the things I have learned about death is that it makes you behave in ways you never thought you would. For example, I have read all your e-mails on your computer, after fiercely guarding them from everyone, fiercely defending your privacy, until one night when I couldn't sleep I gave in and read the few hundred messages that you had sent in the last couple of years.

You would really hate that I did that and I'm sorry. It was only your voice I wanted. I was desperate for it. I didn't bother with the replies.

I come to the cemetery in a kind of ad hoc fashion. Sometimes I pick up a coffee and drink it out there, standing with my back to your gravestone. I like how the sun warms the stone and how the stone keeps the heat a little way into the evening, keeps it longer than the air. It's strange, but when you died and the heat started leaking from your body, it left you at exactly the pace that a stone cools after being in the sun all day. It makes me think that we are made of the natural world after all, attached to it more securely than I had realized.

Your grave is on a slight rise and looks down over a small ravine. In the winter there are bird and rodent tracks in front of your stone. A few times I came out with birdseed to spread on your grave. I liked the idea of the birds landing there and feeding and flying off again. I liked the idea of movement in this place that is so still.

On Christmas Day I drove out and the cemetery

was full of other people clustered round the graves of their loved ones. Some were drinking a toast to their dead. Some had brought flowers and wreaths and small gifts to place in front of the stones. It was comforting to have the company of these other mourners, even though we never said a word to one another.

We planted spring bulbs in front of your grave because you were born in the spring and it will be nice to have flowers opening on your birthday. At the back of your grave we put a small rose bush that has the fragrance of apple blossom. Mum buried your christening mug in front of the stone so that it could be filled with water and hold fresh flowers. I remember your christening mug. It was a good mug to drink apple juice out of when we were children because the metal made the juice taste sharper and kept it cold.

It is hard to know what to do at your grave. Mostly I just stand there and watch the ravine across from me, or the shapes of clouds in the sky. I never know what to say to you there, so I don't say much. It seems irrelevant and weird to speak out loud. On your birthday, Mum and I ate supper by your grave and toasted you by pouring a beer into the ground.

Because you died at the beginning of winter, the earth mound above your coffin couldn't be levelled and grass couldn't be planted there until spring. During that first winter there was this enormous frozen hill of dirt there, with bits of your funeral flowers stuck to it, and small holes where mice had burrowed. It was our raw grief made visible and I rather liked it. It was how I felt, like this earthen monster, badged with wilted roses and bits of green florist foam. Now it's a tidy rectangle of grass, disappointing somehow.

"I just want to dig him up," Mum said the last time we were there together. And I know exactly what she means.

3

On the first page of your last notebook you wrote this:

So today Patrick Swayze dies 1½ years after his initial diagnosis. That maybe gives me until Christmas of 2010.

What do I want to do? Finish my compositions!! Do a recording? Maybe too much to ask.

Travel—London, New York, and something I've never seen, Paris (once more!). Prague, Budapest, and maybe Asia or Cairo.

The only item on that list you got to do was go to New York.

We went together.

It was October, but it felt like spring. The air held a vein of warmth, and we walked around with our coats undone, sat on the steps of the Met in the late afternoon sun.

We had tickets for the opera and the theatre. We went to jazz clubs and museums. It was an exhausting schedule, punctuated with worrying bouts of pain that you could no longer pacify with the constant morphine you were taking by then.

You and I shared a room, as we had often when we were children, and despite the street noise of the city, we slept soundly in our twin beds on the second floor of the hotel. We were both quiet sleepers, waking in the same position that we had fallen asleep in, at the same time, and opening our eyes long before we moved our bodies, watching morning seep through the gauzy curtained window. I had forgotten so many of our childhood similarities. As my younger brother you had always felt so deeply familiar to me that I didn't even register our sameness.

We were three years apart and we grew up as artists together. That was our bond. I was there at the moment you began to play the piano, and you were there for the moment I decided to become a writer. Most of our teenaged years were spent discussing art and our ambitions, huddling together in the covered front porch of our parents' house, smoking cigarettes and enthusing about our dreams. We were both hard workers and stubborn, and in time we largely achieved what we had set out to achieve. It always kept me on my path to know that you were so determinedly on yours.

I thought it would always be that way, that we would grow old doing what we'd always done in our parallel worlds, finally returning to the closeness we'd had as children.

When you first got your dire diagnosis of pancreatic cancer at the end of July, we laughed. *Can you believe it,* you said. *I'm stage 4B, and there is no stage 4C.*

You had been living in Toronto for two years at the time, but were planning to move back to Vancouver and had already rented out your house for this purpose. So, the bad news effectively found you homeless.

You were meant to have lived into the spring, but you died just weeks after we got back from New York. Despite the list titled *Things To Do Before I Die,* you didn't even have time to stop your life enough to absorb fully what was happening to you. You had a full schedule of teaching piano on the day you went into hospital for the emergency operation that killed you.

Stopping a life is harder than it seems, especially a life in full flight. It takes at least three months to bring the whole shuddering freight of obligation and expectation to a halt.

But for now you are not dead. It's the end of October and we're sitting outside at the Lincoln Center. We have tickets for *Aida* tonight, and beforehand we are watching a matinee performance of *South Pacific*. It's intermission and we're eating the sandwiches we bought at the deli where we had breakfast. The sandwiches are already stale, but we're eating them anyway. You are smoking. Since the diagnosis you have taken up smoking again. One of the saddest things in your apartment, when I went to clean it out after you died, was your pack of half-smoked cigarettes with the small blue Bic lighter tucked down the front—the equipment of our youth.

South Pacific was not something either of us had wanted to see. We were there because it fit into our schedule for that day. But the moment the first act started, we turned to each other and said, at the same time, *This is really good.*

So much of theatre and writing and music is sombre, elegiac; the backwards glance, the lovers locked together in the airless tomb. And while this is acceptable when life is good, all that tragedy is hard on someone who is dying. The brightness of

South Pacific cheered us, and at intermission we sat outside and talked about how we didn't want to participate any more in art that was depressing. *Because life is so good,* you said. *We should just celebrate it.*

In the handful of months you had left to live after the cancer was diagnosed, you turned to music with all your best attention. You played piano as much as you could, and you played better than you'd played in years. The music to which you'd given your life sustained you when you were dying. It held you up. It gave you comfort. Your inner world continued to be a rich one, a joyful one, even while your outer world was collapsing.

You stayed in Toronto for the course of chemo, even though you had been waiting to move back out west, your stuff already packed and ready to go. Who knows if staying was the best decision; the chemo didn't really help at all, just made you sicker. But it's hard to stop hoping. It's hard to know when to give up.

You did go back to Vancouver, on November ninth. On November twenty-second you went into hospital, and on December third you were dead.

You sold your piano before you went out to Vancouver, planning to buy another one when you got there, but that never happened. I looked through the last photos in your camera and the final ones are of your piano before you sold it—your piano and your empty piano bench, the sun from the window behind the camera making the keys sparkle.

I liked to listen to you practise when we were young. It was the background noise all through my childhood, and I found it reassuring. The music you made was the essence of you, the best of you, and even when you were thin and weak from the chemo, your playing was as strong as ever.

We all give our lives to something, and our lives are taken from us at some point. We are lucky if what we devote ourselves to can offer us some comfort at the end.

Outside, at the Lincoln Center, intermission was coming to an end. We had finished our sandwiches, and we stood up and walked back into the auditorium. We inched along the row and took our seats. And when the lights went down, and the lights came up, and the music started, we both wanted it to go on forever.

4

The guys next door have removed the solar lanterns that weren't working. I was away for a week and when I came home there was only one lighting the path up to my door. I don't know whether to be grateful or sorry. I sat up in my bedroom last night, looking down at the lone lantern, trying to write and not getting anywhere.

I wanted to give up writing after you died, Martin. There seemed no point to it any more. Maybe because we had grown up as artists together I felt I couldn't go on alone. Or perhaps I just lost my interest in narrative, didn't have the heart for the business of making a story, labouring over consistency and the forward momentum of plot. If I could barely move myself forward through my days, how was I supposed to move a novel along?

For the year after you died, I couldn't even read. All the things that had made up my life, that had been integral to my existence, dropped away, and I was left with just the days, the darkness, the days, and the worst feeling I had ever had, so terrible that it's hard to even call it a feeling. It was more like a cave that I crawled inside. I was made up of nothing but frailties.

I remember when you began playing the piano. You were four and I was seven. I was taking piano lessons from Miss Empringham, a woman in mid-life who thought herself the reincarnation of Beethoven. (I remember her actually saying this.) She lived in an uneasy *ménage à trois* with two other women in what was then a sort of arts colony on the grounds of the Guild Inn, a rambling hotel on a large estate above Lake Ontario. They all lived in a house called Cory Cliff, perched on the edge of the bluffs, and now long gone. There were secret passages in the hotel, and during the Second World War returning servicemen with nervous disorders were treated there. In the 1960s and 1970s it became the Guild of All Arts and the grounds were peppered with cabins and small studios where artists lived and worked. But the time for the arts colony had come and gone. Since the artists had been offered life tenancy, they couldn't be removed. Instead, when they died, their cabins were simply knocked down. Do you remember that Cathy took sculpture lessons from one of the last remaining artists on the property in the 1980s, Elizabeth Fraser Williamson?

Miss Empringham came to our house once a week. She was an avid garbage picker and often brought me something from someone's trash. Sometimes the items still smelled like garbage. One week she brought me an angel formed out of coat hangers and a pair of nylons.

I was, frankly, more interested in Miss Empringham than in the piano. She did look alarmingly like Beethoven, and stamped around, brusque, moody, and impatient. She was often irritated with me, which I rather liked.

You wanted to have piano lessons, but Mum said you were too young, so you asked if you could stay in the living room during my lesson. I didn't want you there as a distraction, or as a witness to my clumsy playing, but Mum said you could stay so long as you were quiet. I remember you sitting absolutely still during my lesson, your hands on your knees, while I squirmed on the piano bench and Miss

Empringham snapped and chided, waving her conductor's wand, or crashing her beefy hands down on the keys.

I don't remember how many lessons you sat through. It couldn't have been very many—maybe two or three—but one day, after Miss Empringham had left the house, you got up from the couch and came over to the piano and played, perfectly, for Mum and I, the piece of music that I had been struggling with all week. After that, Miss Empringham came to the house to teach you, and I was allowed to stop having piano lessons, which was a huge relief.

After you died, some of your friends asked me what you were like as a little boy, and I said serious and sensitive. At the age of five you would walk up the street to the neighbour's house and have tea with her and discuss the Vietnam War. At the age of seven you kept a diary that recorded how many hours a day you were practising the piano, and what competitions you had entered and won, all in shaky childhood script. When we went fishing—which we did a lot as children, left to our own devices at the boat club in Port Perry while our parents worked on their cabin cruiser—you would catch fish, take them off the hook, and kiss them before you threw them back into the water. I think you said something to the fish after you kissed them. *Good luck,* or *Thank you.*

You were deadly serious as a little boy, but as a teenager and man you liked puns and practical jokes. And you were funny. I still have some of the Christmas labels you used to attach to my presents, where you would take the first letters of my name and your name, and make synonymous words from to those letters. *To Handel, Love Mozart. To Heavy, Love Massive. To Hope, Love Mercy.* You did this with everyone in the family, never repeating words or themes from one year to the next.

I never regretted giving up the piano. I much preferred words to music. I loved the world of books, a world I felt was much more exciting than the one I actually lived in. To have some of the thrill of story, I would try to put myself in the way of adventure in my real life. Usually this involved riding my bike around the neighbourhood, or squelching through the pond opposite our house, although neither activity ever yielded anything interesting. For a long stretch of days one summer, I stood at the window of my bedroom, notebook in hand, looking for suspicious people to document. I made you stand with me, as my assistant. Your job was to look up the street while I looked down.

Around this time, I read *Charlotte's Web* by E.B. White. This whimsical story of the friendship between Wilbur the pig and Charlotte the spider moved me as nothing else had moved me before. When that spider died, I was inconsolable. Mum, nonplussed by my sobbing, tried to calm me by pointing out that because Charlotte had babies there were still lots of spiders at the end of the story. But of course these other spiders didn't matter because I didn't know them. I didn't care about them.

Since we lived in the suburbs, few people walked along our street, suspicious or otherwise. Everyone drove everywhere. You soon quit being my surveillance assistant, saying that it was boring. I realized then that it might be better to make up the adventures rather than wait for them to happen to me. And my devastating response to *Charlotte's Web* made me think that if I controlled a story, I would never have to feel that sad again.

I was wrong, but this was how I became a writer.

You said, near the end of being you, that music is always good—meaning, to listen to it, to play it, is always an enriching experience. I can't say the same about writing, and my lifetime of doing it has always held ambivalence and struggle. But it makes sense, if I think back to our beginnings. You responded to the music. You got up from the couch and walked over to the piano and simply entered what had moved you. I looked to writing to provide what life wasn't providing, to be, in a way, a substitute for living. And this has remained. For to write well, to write fully, to really get inside a novel, I have to leave the world I actually live in. I can't have distractions from the story, which means living alone, and creating an environment of calm and routine—wearing the same clothes day after day, eating the same food—so that nothing from the real world interferes with the creation of the fictional one.

Over the years this has worn me down and created a kind of loneliness that is hard to live with, and surprisingly hard to leave.

About ten years ago, when I was writing almost all the time, I remember you saying to me, *You used to do other things besides work,* and I thought that was strange coming from you, who was just as driven to create. But you were right. And now, perhaps, the desire to not write is really just a desire to not leave the real world, a world that has been made possible again, perversely, by your death.

But the thing about writing is that I've done it for so long, I can no longer differentiate where it ends and I begin. My being is enmeshed with what I do. And this is why, in spite of my desire to give up writing, I am writing to you one last time. Writing is what I have, and it's how I make sense of experience.

I even wrote a line at your hospital bedside, as you lay dying, because two ideas occurred to me in that moment and I wanted to remember them. The first was just the very simple fact that, in the end, you can step out of a room or you can't. That is what separates the living from the dying, that one small, enormous action. The second is the poignant truth of the flesh we live inside, that in the end the body leaks or it holds.

Someone is letting off firecrackers tonight. The dog is apprehensive, but she's not scared yet, because she's still so young. We grow into our fears, animals and humans alike. We grow into our fears and our neuroses. So, for now, she sits beside me on the little deck behind my house, panting and nervous, but staying with me.

You had an ulcer at the age of seven. Now the experts say that ulcers are caused by a bacterial infection, but the ulcer always seemed connected to your practising the piano or worrying about your practising. It just felt like further evidence, to me, of your seriousness as a child. And when I look back now, tonight, it seems that neither of us was ever really lighthearted or carefree. We may as well have been adults, not children. We were driven and responsible and pathologically independent.

When we had our last conversation over the phone, as they were wheeling you down the hospital corridor to the operating room, I asked you what you wanted me to do for you, and you said, *You decide what's best. I'll leave it to you. I give in. I give in to the disease. I'll stop working.* And I realized then how hard you'd been fighting, that you hadn't really let anyone help you until that moment—and by then, of course, it was too late.

5

You will want to know what happened to your things because you (like me) were always very attached to your possessions. It gave you comfort to be surrounded by them.

When I went out to Vancouver, when you were first in hospital there, I got your wallet and keys from the nurses and I went to your apartment. It was still a mess because you'd just moved in, just moved back out west two weeks before you went into hospital. There were piles of things all over the floor in the bedroom. The living room was more orderly. The books were on the shelves, the furniture in its place. The pictures weren't yet on the walls, but they were neatly stacked against one wall.

I slept in your sheets, in the bed you'd ordered that had been delivered the day you went into hospital. You called the ambulance in the middle of the night, so you never got to sleep one full night in that bed.

I slept in your bed. I used your towel when I showered. I hauled your laundry—load after load—down to the basement where the washers and dryers were behind a steel door that shushed closed behind me. I did all your laundry and I put your clothes away. I washed your dishes. At night I lay in your bed and stared at the ceiling. Sometimes I slid open the single pane of glass that was your bedroom window and I leaned out over the sill and stared down at the row of cedars that bordered the side of the apartment building and the wooden fence next door. It was late November and there had been a lot of rain. The cedars were wet and aromatic and when I breathed them in, I was reminded of the green and damp smell of England, and I could see how this place reminded you of that one—the England we had, at different times, both lived in—the country where I was born.

I walked through the rooms of your apartment and looked at your belongings. Most of them were deeply familiar. You didn't like to throw anything out, which was a burden when I came back in January to clean out your apartment and jammed garbage bag after garbage bag with outdated microwave instructions, old travel brochures, plastic packaging for various electronics.

But what struck me about your apartment was how little changed your surroundings were from when you were twenty. You had not strayed from our original path, as I had. You still lived a life circumscribed by art. You played the piano, taught the piano, composed at the piano in the day. On the nights you weren't working, you went out with your girlfriend or for a beer with your friends or to sit in a pub and watch the hockey game. Your life could have been the life of an artist a hundred years ago, two hundred years ago. It was only in the last couple of years that you'd owned anything, that you'd tried to be like everyone else—with a car and a house and a debt load—and you'd found it didn't suit you at all. *I'm the kind of person who likes living in an apartment,* you'd said to me.

A lot of your books were the same as mine. I might even have given them to you, but I couldn't remember. I took *English Journey* from the top shelf in the living room and I read a small part of it every night before I went to sleep. If you don't remember, it's the story of a cranky British novelist travelling through the north of England in the footsteps of J.B. Priestley, only she's dragging along a film crew. She spends a lot of the book desperate for a cigarette.

It's a true story. I like that term—*true story.* That's what this is. Because I have ordered experience, that makes it a story. It's as simple as that. While I stand in the chaos and swirl of my life, I am in the midst of truth. Once I decide what experience or sensation comes first, and then what comes second, I have begun to make a story. It doesn't matter that the facts are facts—the ordering of experience is the relevant part.

English Journey was soothing because I'd read it before, years ago, and I knew what to expect from it. Reading it helped me to sleep, helped to calm me down.

At night, after I had spent the day at the hospital, sitting beside your bed, I tidied your apartment. I put anything personal away, kept what was private, private. I phoned your students and cancelled lessons with those who were due to come that week, cancelled the jobs you were set to go to. I downplayed the seriousness of your situation in case you did miraculously recover and would be embarrassed by the dire spin I had put on your prognosis.

This was all before you died, but you wouldn't know this part because you were unconscious.

After you died the decisions were more pragmatic. I kept any piece of paper with your handwriting on it. I threw out everything else. We tried, and mostly succeeded, to sell or give away anything you loved to the people whom you loved. All of us took back from you the things we had given you.

What I kept of yours, aside from what you left me in your will, were strange, small objects: a felt rock that I put in my car, over the cupholder with the loose change in it, which my dog tries to steal every once in a while because it looks like a stuffed toy; a small earthenware jug from your kitchen that sat, empty, on the back of your stove; the donkey finger-puppet from our childhood; your pencils for composing, each one sharpened to a useful, hopeful point; the postcards you bought but never sent, from our last trip together in New York; the books you were reading (one of which was mine; I mean, it was written by me); the CDs from your car; the notes you had made towards pieces of music that you never got to write; some T-shirts; and a cutting board, your champagne glasses, your carry-on bag, a photograph you had bought in New York of Central

Park in winter, a Chopin prelude with your fingering pencilled in, the four bone-handled knives from
your cutlery drawer, one with a chip out of the tip
where you'd clearly used it to try to pry something
open and hadn't necessarily succeeded.

All these objects were small enough to tuck into
the corners of my life.

No one wanted, or could take, your kitchen table,
a wooden one that you'd bought used and painted
with a pale green wash. It was made from tongue-
and-groove panelling that had been nailed onto a
frame with legs. I remember it from every place
you'd ever lived. It was too expensive to ship back
to Ontario, and your friends couldn't find a place
for it in their houses. We had to leave it with your
landlady, who said she'd use it, but I'm not sure
what happened to it in the end because she sold the
building shortly after you died. I'm not sure where
she went.

But we did find out, before she sold the building,
that a brother and sister had rented your apartment.
One of them must be sleeping in your bedroom
right now, in the middle of this night, and the other
sleeping in the room at the front of the apartment
that you were going to use as a music studio.

Your car was sold to a man from Surrey, who came

to look at it with his wife. They were an odd couple. He was large and loud, and had long, stringy hair and pants that he was constantly hauling up with one hand. She was small and quiet, neat in dress and manner. He had agreed to a price on the phone, but once he got to the apartment, he tried to bargain me down. I almost told him to leave because I knew he was getting a good deal on the car and it annoyed me that he would have the gall to try for an even better one. He had brought tools with him, screwdrivers and adjustable wrenches, and he crawled, with great difficulty, underneath the car to check various connections and to make sure it didn't have a rusty underbelly. I stood to the side with his wife, neither of us saying anything, while he huffed and puffed, emerging from under the car with grease marks on his forehead.

When we went for the test drive he finally found something he could use for bargaining. "Look," he said, triumphantly tapping the steering wheel. "The rubber is separating from the metal where the wheel has been gripped too hard." He demonstrated by applying a claw-like pressure to the steering wheel so I could see how the rubber had been pulled away from the metal frame of the wheel. You had bought the car used, so I don't know if it was you or the previous owner who had driven with such a death grip on the steering wheel. I hope it wasn't you.

I gave the man, Clive, a hundred dollars off the price of the car.

Later, we went together to the motor vehicle office to change the ownership. The Vancouver bureaucracy is not the same as the Ontario bureaucracy and required different pieces of paper, none of which we had. I don't remember what we needed to do, only that we were in the office for hours, during which time I had to call Cathy at her job and she had to go to the lawyer's office in Kingston to fax something out to me. (It created a lot of extra work, making us joint executors, because we always had to do bureaucratic tasks in tandem.)

During the lengthy wait, Clive went to the bathroom numerous times, finally coming back to whisper, loudly, to me that he'd just had an operation and now it seemed his stitches had split. "I jammed a whole roll of toilet paper up there," he said, "but I don't think it's going to hold."

I was too weary and dispirited to lose my temper with the motor vehicle employees, but in the end, Clive did it for me. After the umpteenth delay he yelled at the clerk.

"Why can't you be more co-operative? Can't you

see, she's been through enough already!"

I was touched that he said this on my behalf, and when, finally, everything was settled in our favour and we parted company outside your—now Clive's— car, I was actually sorry to see him go.

You would have liked his character, not so much that he was trying for a better deal, but certainly his disdain for the vehicle authorities, so nobly displayed, and the crazy, chaotic state of his innards.

There was no piano for us to sell, as you know, because you had decided to sell your piano before you left Toronto, to avoid the shipping expense. I know you were planning on getting another after you arrived in Vancouver. But when I called you, shortly before you went into hospital, and asked if you'd bought one yet, you said, *I think it will be a while before I get another piano.* It made me uneasy to hear that. For most of your life, from the age of four on, you had played the piano for hours every day. For you to say that meant you were reconciled to your death, already defeated by it. Your not playing the piano in those last two weeks before you went into hospital was more heartbreaking than anything else.

6

My ex-partner, Mary Louise, and I had shared our old dog, Hazel, and after Hazel died, we decided to get new puppies from the same litter. The idea was that we could look after each other's dogs when one of us had to go away. Because Mary Louise was on sabbatical with her partner in Edinburgh until the summer, we decided that I would pick up the two Vizsla puppies from the breeder at the beginning of May and care for them both until she got back in July. Before that, Mary Louise sent me a plane ticket to come and visit her in Edinburgh for her fiftieth birthday in February. I went, but I had just finished clearing out your apartment in Vancouver and I was so tired and weighed down with grief that I could

barely drag myself along behind her as she cheer-
fully marched up and down the hilly Edinburgh
streets, trying to walk me back to life.

You and I had always sent each other postcards when we were away, so I sent you some from
Edinburgh, picking out images that I knew you
would like, telling you things I thought you'd find
interesting or funny. I addressed them to you and
wrote *Vancouver* as the address and dropped them
into the letterboxes unstamped. I didn't think the
dead required postage.

I picked up the puppies the first weekend of May.
I had had an old dog for so long that their energy
was alarming, and even more difficult was the fact
that there were two of them. Our carefully considered plan seemed, initially, to have been a mistake.

Two eight-week-old puppies were almost impossible to control. I had no free time at all, couldn't
leave the house, could barely even leave the room
to shower or eat. I lived on the couch for weeks,
sleeping there at night, sitting there with the puppies in the day. What was surprising was how wild
they were, and also how desperately they tried to
bond with me. They sensed, or knew, how vulnerable they were, that they needed protection, and
they attached themselves to me with a vengeance.

One or the other of them always liked to lie on me,
her heart positioned directly above mine so that our
hearts were beating together.

The dogs are compelled towards one another. I
can't say that they love each other, because sometimes they fight with intent; they have such different personalities that they aren't really compatible.
But they're siblings and that bond seems to trump
all their differences.

I didn't know how I would survive the puppies,
just as I didn't know how I would survive your
death, and in a weird way they were similar experiences, had a similar relentlessness to them.

But now, as I write this, I have just the one dog
to look after, Charlotte. She's a year and a half now,
calmer, easier to tire out. She's sleeping on the rug
after a morning spent racing through the fields with
her sister. We walked through the grounds of an old
estate by the lake and there's a big apple tree there
with the most perfect apples, early apples, ready
now in the middle of August. I picked one and ate
it as I ambled after the dogs through the fields and
the woods. They slept in the car on the way home.
On the way out they had wrestled and fought over
a plastic bag they found under the seat, and stuck
their heads out the window so the wind blew their

lips back and their exposed teeth looked both fierce and comical.

I'm not sure you would like the dogs. You always preferred cats. When I was cleaning out your apartment I found a little framed photo of our childhood cat, Sammy, who was run over by a car outside our house when he was about five. He was magnificent, could stand on his hind legs and rattle doorknobs with his paws, signalling that he wanted out. He had thick glossy black fur and had been found by Cathy when he was young. He was stuck up a tree and she coaxed him down and brought him home draped around her neck like a scarf.

You had a succession of cats in your life, as I've had a succession of dogs. You liked the feline grace of cats. I like the loyalty of dogs, and their crazy exuberance.

I was thinking this morning of all the pets we had when we were children. The different cats who were rescued from dire situations. The dogs with their various neuroses—one afraid to walk on linoleum, one afraid of rubber boots. The seemingly endless parade of fish and turtles and hamsters. The guinea pig who was in love with the rabbit and would try to hop like him around the yard. All of them, eventually, buried at the bottom of the garden in our parents' house in the Toronto suburbs.

When Mum and Dad lived in England, they bred Saint Bernards. I was a toddler when their female dog had her first litter of puppies, and I staggered around the garden at Claygate with the puppies tugging on my clothes or knocking me over. I can vaguely remember the puppies trying to grab my toys through the bars of the playpen, and so I had to mound the toys in the middle of the pen and sit with my arms around them, guarding them, and not being able to play with them at all, as the puppies pushed their heads through the wooden slats.

When we immigrated to Canada, we brought the mother dog, Lisa, with us on the boat. She was too big to go into the shipboard kennels, so the crew kept her up on their deck, where she roamed freely and was fed table scraps.

I loved Lisa, and I think, on some level, I considered myself to be one of her puppies. When we moved into our house in Toronto, she would sleep in the living room by the fireplace, and when I woke in the mornings I would go downstairs and lie up against her belly. I remember that I fitted perfectly between her two sets of paws.

You were just a baby then, so you wouldn't remember any of this. Although maybe you would remember the leather harness that Lisa wore in the winters, and how she would pull us on a wooden sled. She was a big dog—a hundred and fifty pounds—as big as an adult, and that is what I always considered her to be.

Maybe you liked cats because they hung around the piano when you played, kept you company. A cat could sit on the stack of piano music on top of the baby grand in our living room—Mum's piano, her wedding present from her parents that she had shipped over from England when we moved. (The piano that she was always going to leave to you when she died, but which now, of course, she can't.) A cat could sit on the piano and swish her tail to the music, or sometimes step down and delicately walk across the keys.

I think of you playing the piano throughout our childhood, often for eight hours a day. I can still see your thin straight back, your long, dark curly hair, and the arch of your hands over the keys. I hear so many pieces now—on the radio, or through the open windows of city houses—that I recognize from your playing them, although I often have no idea what they are called or who composed them.

And I think that you weren't afraid to die (even though, of course, you didn't want to) because you had spent all those years turning away from a room full of people, turning your body and best attention to the page of notes in front of you. There's something about that particular loneliness that is similar to the loneliness of dying, of leaving a life full of people behind.

Today I went up to fertilize the fruit trees at my cottage, where I'm trying to grow a small orchard. It was raining, which was good because it's been such a dry summer this year, a dry summer following a bitterly cold winter that meant my trees didn't produce any fruit in the spring.

It rained and I mixed the fertilizer with river water and soaked the roots of the trees. The dog ran after frogs, ate something disgusting under a fir tree. I tried to keep an eye on her because sometimes she squeezes under the fence and ends up trotting down the main road. But I guess I let my attention wander because I suddenly heard a sound like thunder and I looked up to see a herd of horses in the field over the river, galloping full tilt, and at the front of the herd was the dog, running like stink. She reached the river first, threw herself in, and swam back to my side, leaving the horses snorting and stamping on the opposite shore.

I am constantly surprised by the moment I'm in.

On the way home I stopped to get some food at the grocery store, and when I came out, I found a small black, plastic horse lying on the sidewalk in front of the store.

When I came with you to chemo in Toronto, that fall after you were diagnosed, I would often drive back to Kingston the same day because of commitments I couldn't shake or alter. You would always give me two of your CDs to listen to on the way home, and I would play them non-stop that week, until I drove back to see you again.

One week, when I was driving home listening to an Oscar Peterson CD you'd lent me, I was about to merge onto the highway when I saw a big green grasshopper crawling up my windshield. It crawled onto the roof of the car, where I could no longer see it. If I got onto the highway, I knew it would be blown off, if it hadn't been blown off already, so I pulled over quickly. I was near the entrance to a park we used to visit when we were young. We rode our bikes there to swim in the creek that flowed out to Lake Ontario. Once, in a rainstorm, when the creek waters were high, your red Queen's Jubilee towel that Granny had sent you from England was swept away. That time too, one of our friends tried to swim across the creek and was rushed downstream in a swirl of white water. He snagged on a tree root in the bank and managed to climb out, a good half mile from where he'd started.

I drove down the hill to the creek and I got out of the car. The grasshopper was still on the roof. I picked it off and put it carefully down in the grass, then I drove back up the hill and onto the highway. When I got home I looked up "grasshopper" and found that it was a symbol of the musician. I took that as a good omen that you would be taken care of by a benign universe. I was desperate for omens.

I told you that story when you came to my house for Thanksgiving. You listened carefully, not moving. When you were listening carefully you never moved a muscle. You listened carefully and you said, *You saved me.*

Your response made me realize how irrefutable birth order was. I would always be your older sister, and it would always be my job to protect you— your job to believe that I could. When I got home from the cottage today I looked up the symbolism of the horse. In some cultures, the horse is seen as a mediator between heaven and earth, between the dead and the living.

7

You would have liked your memorial. It was held at the dance studio in Toronto where you used to play for ballet classes. You spent years playing for such classes, both in Toronto and in Vancouver, but this studio was the one where you spent the most time, where you had the longest history. The owner of the studio was a close friend of yours.

White curtains had been hung at the back of the stage area. There was a podium and a piano. Across the front of the room was a long trestle table filled with food. Everyone had brought something. There was wine and mineral water. Your CDs of Chopin and Janéček had been reissued and were for sale. There was a slideshow projected onto a blank wall, photos of you as a child and as a man. It was hard not to stand in front of the images as they flickered past, wanting to see you again and again.

So many people came. It would have made you happy to see how many loved you and wanted to remember you. Even our childhood neighbours came, those children we used to build forts with and skate with on the pond opposite our house. Everyone looked remarkably the same, as though forty-odd years were nothing at all.

Your ex-students played the piano, one—who has become a concert pianist herself—so brilliantly that it made everyone forget, for an instant, that you were dead. A little ballet student danced for you. She was only about six years old, but had wanted to do something in memory of you. She called you *Mr. Martin.* You were her first death, and her dance was sweet and sad, a little halting in parts where she forgot her footing or became overwhelmed for a moment by the crowd.

We all said something short. No one wanted to start crying in the middle of a speech. Your first employer, from another ballet studio, talked about how you'd applied for the job when you were four-teen and she'd doubted that you were old enough for the work, but you convinced her otherwise, and she was not sorry she'd hired you. (We worked young, remember? We had paper routes from the age of ten, and part-time jobs from fourteen.) You wouldn't like the fact that the church that housed that ballet school is now being turned into condos. I drove past it just last week and the hoarding was up all around the building.

Some people couldn't talk. Your friend Ward stood at the back of the room in his suit, tears running down his face. You and he looked the most alike, remained looking like your younger selves, with your masses of curly hair. You wouldn't have wanted Ward to be so sad, but I think it would have touched you to see how hard he cried.

I talked about how I'd been looking through your address book after you died, trying to find the numbers for people who needed calling and I came across an entry under *S* for *Steve. Nice guy on flight from L.A. who's going through a hard time.* It struck me how *you* that was, to strike up a conversation with a stranger and take his number. And that you would have called Steve at some point, maybe late at night, after work, to check in and see how he was doing. Because you genuinely cared about people—strangers as well as friends. And this is what I said, that the empathy that made you such a brilliant musician also made you an extraordinary human being.

Even that last phone conversation we had, as you were being wheeled into the operating theatre at the hospital, was as much about me as it was about you.

I remember that conversation so clearly because when the phone rang, I was just pulling up in front of my house in Kingston. I had already had the call early that morning that you'd been admitted to hospital, because the cancer in your abdomen had eaten through your intestine and ruptured your bowel. I had already booked my flight to get out to Vancouver the following day. As I parked my car outside my house, the surgeon told me you needed an emergency operation. I told her to pass along the message that I'd be there tomorrow, and to tell you I loved you, and she asked if I wanted to talk with you. At the time I thought this was a generous thing for her to do, to get a portable phone and patch us through, and it surprised me—but now I can see they were worried you would die on the operating table.

That conversation was full of logistics, as almost all of our conversations were. We were always trying to figure out how to get what we wanted in motion. I needed to find out what you wished me to do about your situation. You needed to say how you wanted things handled. We were both afraid you would die, although neither one of us mentioned death. But I kept saying "Goodbye" when I meant to say "See you tomorrow." And you said, *Make sure you have a good life.*

Your empathy was so acute that you would enter a room full of people and immediately be attracted to the most needy, the one with the highest emotional temperature. And so your own needs were often neglected in favour of pleasing others. But I'm glad you said those words to me, almost the last words you spoke, because I think about them all the time. I *am* trying to have a good life, although I'm not always sure how to go about this.

When you were dying, after we'd had the mach-ines unhooked and the breath was struggling out of you, I put my forehead against yours because I thought that I could absorb the last bit of life from you and take you in through my skin, that in that moment, and going forward, you could continue to live through me. But instead what happened was that a part of me went with you, swift and unrecoverable.

This past week I was canoeing in Algonquin Park, something I do every summer, something I love to do. It was a mixed trip, some rain and a great deal of wind in the first part of the week, and then a perfect, sunny day near the end. We saw a moose and heard the wolves howling; we lay out on a rock by the water and watched the first stars spark in the August night sky.

On the way back, over the last portage, Charlotte cut her paw. At first it seemed like nothing, and when I put her in the car at the access point, after the gear had been loaded in and the canoe strapped to the car roof, I didn't give it another thought. She was exhausted from living outdoors all week and slept soundly in the back seat. I was driving out of the park, listening to politician Jack Layton's funeral on the radio. He died of cancer too, and it was difficult not to think of you when he went so quickly. You were the first person I wanted to call after he died, because you liked him and had voted for his party. I was listening to the funeral, a state funeral because he died in office as the leader of the official opposition, something else you didn't live to see but would have appreciated. I was listening to the funeral and driving out of the park and I looked back to see how the dog was doing and she was sitting in a pool of blood.

I drove to the Freshmart in the tiny town of Whitney, because I thought I could buy something there to bandage Charlotte's paw. Inside the Freshmart I asked the woman in the produce department if she knew of a vet nearby. She said the cashier had a sister who was a vet. The cashier called her sister, who worked at a practice an hour away, and the sister phoned the vet on call for me and I made an arrangement to meet him at the clinic.

The dog had to have an emergency operation because her paw had been cut so deeply she'd severed a vein. Because there was no vet tech, I had to help with the sedation, holding Charlotte's head up when she was unconscious so the vet could put a tube down her throat for oxygen, holding the mask over her face.

She tried to fight the sedation, as you had tried to fight yours, twitching and shaking her head to clear the confusion. The vet had to use more than the normal amount of anesthetic. "She's a fighter," he said. "Look how she's fighting me every step of the way."

I wept over the prone body of the dog, her tongue hanging out of her mouth, her head lying in a puddle of drool. I had to step out of the room when the vet put the ten stitches in her paw. She wasn't in danger of dying, but I felt that she would die, and this, I think, is the legacy of your death, is part of how it lives on in me—that I will be, and am, brought to my knees any time something bad happens to a person or a creature that I love. I can't stop myself from fearing the worst, because the worst has happened.

8

The solar lanterns have gone from the front walk-
way. They appeared, and now they've disappeared.
No explanations for either action. The garden out
front is full of weeds, but I find it hard to care. I
haven't lived in this house long enough to consider
that garden to be my garden. I didn't plant any of
it.

I went past your old house in Toronto twice. The
first time was just before it sold. I could see the
mass of black-eyed Susans in the front garden, out
of control and filling every square inch. Wild and
beautiful and probably in violation of some neat-
ness bylaw. The little bungalow looked the same as
when you had lived there, and it felt as if I could

just knock on the door and you would open it and say, *Hey, Helen,* as you always did. You would open the door and I would follow you down the narrow hallway to the kitchen, and then out through the dining room and your bedroom to the back garden. The house had such a strange layout—like a train carriage, I said when you bought it, and I think I hurt your feelings. But it was one long corridor with rooms off that corridor and a weird addition at the back of the house that included a dining room with a vaulted ceiling and skylight, but no other windows, and a room behind that, with sliding doors onto the garden, which had to be a bedroom because there was no other bedroom in the house. But it became public space because it was the only way to access the yard from the house. You bought the house for the space, and because the front room was large and separate from the rest of the house and could be used as a piano studio, to teach from and practise in. You bought it because your girlfriend was thinking about coming out to Toronto to live with you.

The second time I went past your house was this spring. I had been avoiding driving by, but it was a sunny day and I felt like I could handle whatever sad feelings the sight of your old place would stir up. I was prepared for that, but I wasn't prepared for what I saw—a brand new, big, ugly house on the site of your little white bungalow. Your house had been knocked down, was entirely gone, not even a single black-eyed Susan left standing sentinel in the front garden.

One night I looked back through my address book and counted up all the places you'd lived (16), and then all the places I've lived (17).

Our parents never moved and yet we moved all the time. Maybe one was the result of the other, or maybe, and more likely, our nomadic existence was due to changes in fortune and relationships.

I liked the times we lived near each other in Toronto, when we were in our twenties and early thirties. The city was different then, less commodified, grittier. Artists, not young investment bankers, lived in the lofts, and the loft spaces were big and drafty with no real kitchen and a bathroom down the hall that was shared with bikers and junkies. There were old hotels downtown where one could buy cheap trays of draft beer in the afternoons. Factories had been abandoned but not yet pulled down or redeveloped, and all over the city were the ghosts of the industry that had once fuelled it. I particularly liked the old Inglis plant, with its land bridge over Strachan Avenue. In the late 1930s women munitions workers there built Bren guns and Browning 9-mm pistols.

I remember your basement apartment in the east end of Toronto that repeatedly flooded, and where mice used to swing on the cord to your kettle, and at night you would wake up and hear the sound of live mice eating the dead ones caught in the traps.

I remember the apartment on Palmerston near Queen with the huge kitchen that you painted yellow—the house in Staines, England, where it was so cold that when I visited I had to sleep in gloves and a hat—the upstairs apartment on Oxford Street in Kensington Market that you shared with your old girlfriend and her orange cat, Charles.

We worked at various jobs, lived in our largely crappy apartments with our partners, and devoted as much time as we could to becoming better artists. When we saw each other it was on the fly, between my three part-time jobs or the commitments in your relentless teaching schedule. We would meet for a beer or a coffee. Sometimes we would go to a movie or a play. We would meet and talk about ideas, what we were working on, what we were thinking about and reading, whom we were currently influenced by. We were purposeful, and when I found some of my old letters in your apartment and looked through them, I saw how optimistic and happy I was then and it startled me to meet that youthful version of myself and realize that I had become less happy through the years, not more.

You always liked moving. It signalled a fresh beginning and you would be full of hope for the life that your new place would offer up. Even at the end, crazy as it was to move three thousand miles when you were dying, you embarked on yet another fresh start, renting an apartment in a building where you'd lived before. You spent your last good energies unpacking your stuff, putting books on shelves, and getting your kitchen in order. You had complete disregard for the cancer, didn't really change anything about your life to accommodate the disease. Everyone—your doctors, your friends, your family—got angry with you for not taking better care of yourself. You wouldn't do even the simplest of things—drink more water to offset the effects of the chemo. *Sure,* you'd say, if one of us nagged you about drinking water; but then you wouldn't do it. You'd agree to everything and do nothing.

You kept working, because you needed the money and because you liked your work, liked to play and teach the piano. You kept up your brutal schedule, working seven days a week, never having regular mealtimes and sometimes not eating for an entire day. You thought you could live to the outside edge of the potential lifespan of the disease—two years— and if that was the case, you had plans to slow down later and then do some of the things you wanted to do that weren't about working—composing and travelling, mainly.

Of course, none of this happened.

When I look back on it now, I find your giving the disease no purchase admirable. A little foolish perhaps, but mostly admirable. You died on your feet, as it were, and I respect that. I hope that I do the same.

I'm not afraid to die, you said. *I just don't want to.*

And when you asked my opinion about whether you should move back out west, I said, "Go," without any hesitation at all. We still need something to dream on, even when we're dying. We still need plans, even when we're out of time. We still need to feel alive.

I called you one day, shortly after you'd flown west, and you were distraught, standing in the middle of all your boxes, exhausted, in the new and empty apartment. *I think I've made a terrible mistake,* you said. Later that day, or the next day, you called back and said your friends had come over to help you unpack and you felt better, that everything was looking good and you were happy.

But when the emergency room doctor called me early on a late November morning to say that you'd been admitted to the hospital with a perforated bowel, he said you'd told him you came back out to Vancouver to die.

Of all the places in Toronto I associate you with, the old Royal Conservatory building on Bloor Street is the one that has the most meaning for me. You went to school there, on a music scholarship at the age of sixteen, to study performance and composition for a year before moving to London to study with Peter Katin.

The Conservatory building, built in the late 1880s of decorative red brick, Medina sandstone, and polished granite, is both ornate and functional, a combination true of a large number of the city's Victorian institutions. But the most enjoyable aspect of the building wasn't the imposing facade, but rather what lay behind the Conservatory: Philosopher's Walk, the winding path that was once an old riverbed and connects Bloor Street to Hoskin Avenue and the university. The practice rooms were at the back of the building, and when I strolled past on a summer night, I could hear notes from different pianos, and voices opening and closing through the windows of the Conservatory. If I were meeting you, I would often sit on a bench on Philosopher's Walk, listening to the impromptu concerts occurring simultaneously in the air above the grass and street lamps, above the winding path between the trees. The new Conservatory, with its envelope of glass, seems less intimate. There's no music leaking out.

Death feels a bit like the vanished city, like wandering through a landscape I used to recognize but that has now been radically altered. It was a mistake to think that life was solid ground under my feet, and that every day I would be able to step back down onto the same earth. To have you gone—you, who went clear to the bottom of my world—has thrown everything off balance, has left me wandering like a ghost in my own life.

9

I turned fifty this spring, an age you'll never reach. I missed getting a card from you, although Cathy sent me a card you would have sent to me, and when I saw it in the mailbox I thought for a second that you had managed somehow to escape being dead for an hour or two and had gone out to buy it for me. The last card I have from you was for my forty-eighth birthday. You said on that card that you were proud to have me as a sister. This surprised me because we usually sent each other mocking messages about getting older. Because of that card, I sent you a sentimental image of several mice for your birthday in May, the sort of illustration we would have liked in one of our children's books.

Over the years we stopped giving each other presents for birthdays, but you probably would have given me something for my fiftieth. A present from you was always something to be cherished because you chose so thoughtfully. I still have almost everything you ever gave me.

I turned fifty and I had a party. My new house was full of people and everything was a blur of sound. The two dogs came to the party, and I looked over at some point to see them sitting very still on the couch, overwhelmed, their ears flattened back on their skulls by the barrage of noise.

I had a party because I felt that my life had been hollowed out and I wanted to fill it back up. I had this idea that the people who came to my house on the night of my birthday would be the people who would go forward with me into the next part of my life. It was a bit superstitious to feel that way, but there's been a lot of magical thinking going on since you died, for everyone. Mum keeps thinking you're turning on the radio at her cottage. "Why would he care about turning on the radio?" I ask her. But I'm no better. There was a sundog in the sky on the day of your funeral, and there was one in the sky on my birthday, and it was hard not to think it was you.

Mum recorded your phone message and gave me

the tape, along with a CD of you practising Mozart, stopping and starting the same pieces in a way that is so familiar and comforting. Your voice on the phone message is strong and you enunciate every word in case potential students are calling for lessons. In the first couple of months after you died, I used to call your old number and then hang up before a new person could answer. It still feels as though I could just call you, Martin, or that one day the phone will ring and it will be you on the other end. When I was still out in Vancouver cleaning your apartment, and Mum had arrived too, we went to lunch with your Mexican friend, Isaac, and he was telling us how, in Mexico, loved ones leave a bowl of fruit out for the dead, and light a small fire at the front door so that their spirits will be able to find the way home. In the morning, Isaac said, the fruit will still be in the bowl, but if you go to take a bite of it, all the juice will have been sucked out.

Perhaps I minded those tacky solar lanterns disappearing because they were like fires that could have welcomed you back.

10

After you died I started playing badminton again, regularly and with determination. It was our sport when we were young. We played through the week and on Saturdays. One summer we went to badminton camp in Oakville, where we did drills for the better part of the day, then played matches, and then, at the very end, ran five miles.

You were better than I was, partly because you were younger and could play in a lower age category. You were so good that one year you won the Ontario championship for Under 14s. The boy you beat went on to become a member of the Canadian Olympic team. You could have been that good, but you had to choose between badminton and piano, and you chose piano. There's only so much room in a life for serious pursuits.

I play badminton here at the gym on the army base. Civilians can use this gym and pay per use, and this suits me better than joining a club because I'm often away and don't have regular weeks.

I play with Anne, who had cancer herself a couple of years ago. We're evenly matched, although both of us are well past our prime. I'm a good forty pounds heavier than I used to be when you and I played as children, and so I have to rely on careful shots rather than speed. But my body still knows what to do, and sometimes, just for a moment, when I hit a smash or manage to do a graceful drop from the back line, I am inside my sixteen-year-old body again. Perhaps we cleave to the repetition of actions because we're looking to find ourselves where we once were; and sometimes this body remembers how to talk to that body, through the static of the years.

11

It's a beautiful summer night, warm, just a little wind. I took the dog for a walk around the block with her bandaged foot. She's stopped limping, but I can't let her off leash yet and we're both bored by her incarceration.

I'm not writing this in my office, a nice square room on the second floor of this house that I don't seem to use for anything other than storing my books. It has my desk (which is Granny's old kitchen table) and a chair, a nice view out over the trees of the neighbourhood backyards, but I can't seem to settle there. When I first moved into this house, that was the room I slept in. I would lie on a mattress on the floor and look out at the dark patch of sky between the houses. Often I couldn't sleep. Often I woke up not knowing where I was.

This still happens. I wake up and don't recognize this place as home, don't recognize this life as my own. I have to shake my head, the way the dog shook her head to clear the fogginess of the anesthetic.

I write from a chair in my bedroom at the front of the house on the second floor. I look down into the front garden and the street. I hear the voices of the men next door on their porch. When the moon is up I can see the cross on the roof of the church across the road.

I have a little table by the chair with a couple of books on it—a notebook with notes that I made when you were dying and shortly afterwards, and a big hardcover book called *The Apples of New York, Volume I*. Above the table is a framed photograph of two trees on either side of an old stream bed. I took this photograph about thirty years ago and gave it to you, and you hung it in every house you lived in, often over your piano.

The photograph is from Exmoor in England. It's from a short walking holiday we took when we were young. Even though the film quality isn't good and the sky has completely washed out to white, I can remember that day, distantly, in the same way that

I suppose one day I'll remember you. I remember that it was sunny, that the sky was blue, that we were walking through the moor and were full of the energy of youth and we were happy. I don't know what you remembered from that photograph, and I wish now that I'd asked you.

The stream bed is the path. The stones are bare, but look slick with moisture. Maybe it was early in the morning and the world was still damp with dew. There are banks on either side of the stream bed, overgrown banks of tangled vegetation that probably cover stone walls. The two trees grow out of, or behind, those banks, and their branches reach out through the air above the stream bed and entwine with one another, creating an arch through which I can see the green fields that lie before us.

12

We travelled a lot together when we were young. When I was in my early twenties, I went to live in England. It was my plan to spend a year there, writing a novel in a disciplined way, and if I could do that, I felt, I could dedicate my life to being a writer.

It wasn't a bad plan, really, inspired no doubt by tales of the American and British writers who went to live in Paris in the 1930s. It seemed romantic to be heading overseas to become a novelist, even though my situation was a great deal less romantic than Hemingway's or the Fitzgeralds'.

I went to live with Dad's mother in Forest Row, a sleepy little village filled with the elderly at the edge of the Ashdown Forest near East Grinstead.

It seemed a good fit as Granny was getting old and wanted someone in the house to keep an eye on her, and I had very little money, not enough to pay the rent on lodgings of my own. I lived with Granny for free, in exchange for doing errands for her and some light cooking, and generally making sure that she didn't have a fall and lie, undiscovered, in the house for weeks.

The house was Dad's childhood home. It had a name, remember—Ashcroft—and it was a large, Tudor-style house on an acre of grounds, with a massive green hedge at the front that flopped over and lay in the front garden like a great, green whale. You never spent much time in that house, just the odd afternoon for the obligatory visit when we were over in England as a family. Granny did not particularly like children and we were often bored there, escaping the house whenever possible to go up the road to the Ashdown Forest and kick a ball through the bracken.

I slept in Dad's old room, which was part of the attic, a room full of angles and corners. There were three large windows that opened out over the garden and I would sometimes sit on the sill at dusk, smoking, one leg dangling outside because there were no screens on the windows; they simply opened out into the soft English air that often smelled of burning leaves.

The bed was cold and damp. I was never warm enough in England, even in good weather. I remember in your house in Staines you used to place hardcover books upright at the end of the bed to hold all the bedclothes up. Otherwise, when you were lying on your back, the weight of the blankets and eiderdown were too great.

I slept in Dad's room, and I had the dining room, which was directly underneath, as my study. It too overlooked the back garden. It had a dark blue carpet and an old sideboard that rattled when I walked past. I wrote at the massive oak dining table that was no longer used to eat from as Granny now had her meals on a tray in the living room. I wrote with my back to the garden so I wouldn't be distracted and I faced a large oil painting on the far wall of Dad when he was a child. In it he was meant to be sitting on a bench, but he had one leg stretched towards the floor and I could tell he was in the process of trying to escape while the painting was being made. It was much more distracting to look at that painting than it would have been to gaze out the window at the garden.

In the corner of the room was a small fireplace

where I burned the great heap of coal that had been in the cellar since the Second World War. It was always freezing in that room, even with the fire going.

I was lonely in England. Granny and I had an alliance of sorts, but she was not a sympathetic companion. She preferred silence to talk, her own company to anyone else's. She read the *Daily Telegraph* from cover to cover every morning. If it was sunny, she read the paper in the solarium at the side of the house, which overlooked the small orchard. If she was feeling energetic, she went out and deadheaded the roses. In the afternoons she liked to watch horse-racing on TV. Sometimes she was visited by a neighbour, and the moment the woman left, Granny would make disparaging remarks about her. I remember one woman, a widow from up the road (there was a large number of war widows on Ashdown Road in those days), coming into the living room one morning and dancing about, saying, "I've been up on the forest, Marjorie. Feel my hands," and thrusting her arms towards Granny and forcing Granny to do something she felt awkward doing, to touch another human being. After the neighbour had gone, I remember Granny saying, "She's completely off her head. Quite mad. Don't let her in next time she comes."

All morning I worked on my novel. In the afternoons I went out into the world and walked, doing errands in the little village, or walking three miles up the hill to East Grinstead, or out on the forest. There seemed to be old people everywhere in that village, no one my age, and I was too shy to talk to anyone even if there had been. Some days I didn't speak at all. Once a week I went up to London and wandered around, went to galleries and bookstores. Once a week I took a bus the ten miles to Tunbridge Wells and visited Mum's parents—the "good grandparents," as we called them—in their rented house in Langton Green. I used their typewriter to type up what I had written on my novel that week. They fed me supper and we watched something on TV, and then they drove me back to Ashcroft.

Most nights I made supper for Granny and myself and wheeled it in from the kitchen on the two-level gold-coloured metal tray that she kept parked by her chair in the living room. Supper was always a variation of the same thing—potted meat on toast or a boiled egg, with an apple for Granny at the end and a pear for me.

I read a lot. I smoked a great deal. I wrote letters home and waited for the mail with a fierce hopefulness. At Christmas I went to visit Mum's sister and her family, where I saw a giant chicken out back of their house and thought I had drunk too much wine until I realized it was a neighbour's amateur topiary effort.

You and I made plans to travel through Europe after your school year ended, and I counted down the days until I was able to go and pick you up from the airport in my rented blue Ford Cortina. I hadn't been able to sleep at all the night before you arrived and left ridiculously early for Gatwick, scraping the frost from the windshield of the car in the dark with a spatula.

I was probably happier to see you walk through those arrival gates than I've ever been to see anyone.

I had run out of money by the time you got to England, and so we travelled through Europe on your student loan, which we then spent the next few years paying back. You wanted to visit the composers' houses and gravesites, and so this is mainly what we did, discovering a multitude of apartments in Vienna where Mozart or Beethoven had lived, going to Wagner's house at Tribschen, standing by the Danube where Schumann had thrown himself in to drown out the voices in his head. We slept in youth hostels, and on the train as we were travelling from place to place. Sometimes, to save on accommodations, we slept on park benches in the day. We

ate bread and cheese, and gorged on hostel break-
fasts that often included cold meat and hard-boiled
eggs. In France, on the way back to England, you
got food poisoning and threw up continually into
the flowered wastepaper basket in our rented room.
You asked me to go and find you a doctor, but I told
you that you'd be all right without one, because my
French was so poor that I had no idea how to go
about finding a doctor, or, if I did find one, how we
would pay for it. I was awake all that night, worrying
that you would die because I hadn't gone in search
of medical aid.

We were cavalier with our itinerary, staying only a
couple of nights in most places, figuring that we'd be
back to the larger cities many times in our adult lives.
With the exception of Paris and Vienna, I haven't
returned to a single place we visited all those years
ago.

A good friend of mine says that one should do
what one most wants in the morning, because a day
always gets away from you. Life is like that too, and if
you don't do things when you're young, it gets harder
and harder to do them as you accumulate responsi-
bilities and ties. I wish I'd known that then.

13

We finally went to Paris together again the summer
before you received your diagnosis. I had to go there
to research my latest novel and, on a whim, I asked
you to come with me. You had just arrived in Toronto
and I hadn't seen much of you. My life had become
so busy that it had been hard to factor you back into
it. I think you were finding this with many of your
friends, that you'd been gone from the city for thirteen years, and in that time people had just got on
with their lives.

The geographical space for those thirteen years
between your life and mine had made us distant.
I presumed our old intimacy, but I don't think it
existed in the same way. We had both turned towards

the people in our lives who were present, and so your life was largely the one you had made for yourself in Vancouver. We still talked on the phone, and I still felt that I could say anything to you and you would understand, but not having regular physical contact meant that we were not as close as we once had been. Often you would call me just as you were on your way out, which would completely exasperate me, but I can see now that although you still wanted the connection, you didn't want to spend any time on it. And frankly, it was the same for me.

But Paris was good. It felt easy to travel with you, so familiar that it didn't require much thought or negotiation. We had a sweet little hotel room with twin beds on a quiet street in the area of Paris where my novel takes place. Your side of the room was a heap of clothes and pieces of paper. (You always overpacked.) My side was neat—a small pile of books and my knapsack. I didn't unpack. You unpacked immediately and used up all the drawers.

Every morning we went around the corner to a café for breakfast. Then I headed off to research a building, or an area, or a street, or visit a museum— I had a careful list of all the places I needed to see in the two weeks we were there—and you walked over to the Louvre. You had decided to spend all your time there, visiting a different room every day.

In the evenings we would sometimes meet up, but you had friends in Paris and would visit them as well. When we did go out together you were distracted, as you often were, not listening to anything I said, or talking right over me, never making eye contact. If I wanted to tell you anything important, I had to say it all in a burst, so that there might be a chance of your hearing some of it. This was wearying, and once I was standing on the street near our hotel and I saw you hurrying past, and I didn't call out to you. It seemed easier in that moment not to, and I watched you as a stranger might—a tall, thin man with long, dark curly hair, dressed in loose black jeans and an old T-shirt, walking briskly back to the hotel with a painting under your arm that you'd just bought from a street artist near Notre-Dame.

But we slept in the same quiet way, awakened at the same time in the morning. From our twin beds we talked as we used to. You told me a secret you'd been carrying around for years. I told you how I really felt about the relationship I was currently in.

In a tiny shop near the Métro, I bought a bronze sparrow. It was the only thing I wanted and I placed it on the table beside my hotel bed so that the still, round bird was the first thing I saw every morning. The plumpness of it reminded me of the middle-aged figure of Sainte-Beuve, the poet I was writing about in my novel.

One of your friends from Paris called me the day you died, having just heard that you were in hospital. I held my phone up to your ear so that she could talk to you, and I could hear her crying. The nurses had given you a lot of sedation because you fought if you weren't completely knocked out, tried to get rid of the tubes and the needles and the ventilator that tentacled your body. You were young and strong and when you struggled it was in earnest.

This was the day you were going to die, the day we were going to let them unhook you from the machines, because we had been told that you likely had brain damage from liver failure—a direct result of your compromised liver having to process the drugs they used to keep you sedated.

But when I held that phone to your ear and your friend talked to you from Paris, you thrashed your head back and forth, strained to open your eyes, pursed your mouth and flexed it, not unlike the way the fish you'd caught when we were children looked when they were out of water for a few moments and gasping for breath.

It was clear you were trying to communicate. It was clear you wanted to say something back through the phone line, but I could do nothing to help you. I took the phone away from your ear.

"He heard you," I said to the sobbing voice on the other end. "He heard everything you said."

14

I'm in Italy, at a literary festival, in a small northern Italian town surrounded by three lakes and with a small river running through the centre of the town. It goes without saying that you would like it here, Martin, but I'll say it anyway.

The bed and breakfast where we're staying is sixteenth century. My room is huge and has windows that open above a busy street. This morning there was a market and I awoke to the sounds of people bargaining at the stalls. The boards on the floor of the room are two feet wide, and the windowsill is so deep that I have to stand on tiptoes to lean over and see into the street below. In the big reception room that is next to mine, the ceiling is covered with frescoes—entwined leaves and the garlanded heads of classic Roman men. There is also a huge chandelier that droops down into the centre of that room. All the decoration is from the top down and there is nothing but a simple tiled floor below. Out back there is a little courtyard with trees and birds, a glimpse of sky between the branches. The back wall of the house is open to this courtyard and at night, when the lamp is turned on in the hallway, bats fly in to circle the light.

My event today was, strangely enough, at a music conservatory. I was interviewed outside, in the courtyard, and all the while that I was listening to my interviewer speak in Italian on one side of me, or my translator whisper in English on the other side of me, I could hear music tumbling from the windows behind me—strings, and then later, a piano. I wonder if there will come a day when that will not make me think of you.

It was hard to remain calm on the first bumpy flight over from Canada, and the second bumpy flight from Frankfurt to Bologna. I am both more and less afraid of dying since you died. I am less afraid of the actual event, but more afraid that it will happen sooner than I want it to—as was the case with you. Being in a strange place makes me feel untethered to my life back home, and that in turn makes me feel nothing but panic—which is the feeling I had all fall when you were dying. It is easy now for one state to echo another.

Last night we went to the restaurant in Mantova where Virginia Woolf ate when she was here in 1921. I had the local specialty—tortellini stuffed with pumpkin and amaretto. It was very good. Apparently Virginia Woolf also liked it when she ate there, all those years ago.

I was thinking today about how, when you travelled, wherever you went, you used to have to find a piano to practise on. European cities were good for this because there was always a church or a theatre or a music school that would let you use theirs. That was not an unusual request for them. It could easily have been your piano that I heard behind me when I was talking at the conservatory today. Sometimes, when we were together in another city, I wrote for a few hours while you went off and practised on some borrowed piano. I liked meeting you after you'd been playing because you were always happy and ready for adventure.

Later on today we went to visit the palace that is on the edge of one of the three lakes. Again, the decoration was top-heavy, all those ceiling frescoes and nothing on the walls. But someone explained to me that there had been decorations on the walls once — tapestries, leather hangings — and they had, of course, been removed by various owners who had wanted to hang other artworks in their place. It's harder to change the thing you cannot reach, so the ceiling decorations have largely remained untouched.

In one of the rooms hornets were boiling in the loins of the entwined plaster lovers on the vaulted ceiling. In another room — the most important room of the palace, where the prince entertained visiting dignitaries — on each of the four walls there were life-size portraits of the prince's favourite horses. One was called *Gloriosa.* They all looked plump and happier than any of the people in the palace paintings. And in the room with the frescoes of giants that started at the floor and covered all the walls there was graffiti dating from the sixteenth century. Apparently all we ever want to do is affirm our presence, as the graffiti was just names carved into the plaster walls. And there was your name, *Martinus,* and the date, *1730 AD,* on a giant's white thigh.

This afternoon I went to hear Virginia Woolf's niece speak. She's ninety-three, has the vacant stare of the elderly. Dad has that expression these days, especially since you died — a look of innocent confusion, almost childlike. The niece was on a panel with two academic experts on her aunt. They both talked for a long time about the importance of Virginia Woolf as a writer. Then they asked the niece to talk about this too. All she could say was that Virginia Woolf was a good aunt, and that she hadn't read all of her books because, when she was young, her family never thought her aunt was a very good writer.

It's hard to be objective about someone you know. And really, how could the niece of Virginia Woolf talk about the writing without going through the filter of her relationship to her aunt? Maybe the more real thing is simply to say what she said, that Virginia Woolf was *amusing*, that she was *nice*.

It was almost a day coming home, what with the various flights and a layover in Munich. The jet lag was bad, although it was hard to even recognize it as jet lag because it felt exactly like grief—complete exhaustion and a kind of dislocation from my surroundings. It's how I've been feeling pretty much every day for a year and a half now. It's strange that jet lag and grief should feel so much alike, although it makes a kind of sense too.

15

The last time I was in Germany I was at the
Frankfurt Book Fair, promoting one of my earlier novels. I was going to be interviewed, in tandem with an American writer, by a local celebrity
known simply as "The Stag." The Stag was a man
in late middle age who had lived in the woods near
a nuclear facility for a year, protesting the use of
nuclear power and its potentially catastrophic effect
on the surrounding humans and animal life. The
Stag had dressed as a deer, complete with antlers
and attired head to toe in buckskin. He gambolled
through the trees. Sometimes the press came to the
woods to interview or photograph him. Once a day
his supporters brought him food and supplies.

The Stag sat between the other author and me at a table on a stage at the front of a long room filled with journalists and others, most of whom were there primarily to see The Stag, who, although he no longer lived in the woods, still enjoyed celebrity status.

When the event began, The Stag leaned into the microphone and said, "I haven't read either of these books, and I have nothing to say about them."

The other author, a woman around my age, shot me a panicked look across the table, and in the awkward moments that followed, I know we were both desperately thinking of how to save ourselves.

We ended up interviewing each other while The Stag played with the fringes on his buckskin jacket, looking completely bored, and he bolted the moment our allotted hour together was up.

I don't think that I ever told you this story, but you would have loved the idea of a middle-aged man leaping through the forest dressed as a deer, and his refusal to co-operate at the event would have made you laugh.

16

I've been thinking about the human soul, about the presence of the unseen in our lives, about how, the moment you died, I felt you leave. What was it that left? And why did I feel that you did leave? It wasn't simply that a light was turned off, that your consciousness was stopped, but rather that you moved swiftly from your dead body and went somewhere else. But where did you go?

That's the real question, I guess, and one we all keep asking, even now, a year and a half later.

We weren't raised with religion, but you were probably the most religious of us all, mainly because you spent a lot of time inside churches. As you would probably be the first to point out, churches usually have good acoustics. You played concerts in churches. You practised there. You accompanied church choirs. Inadvertently, you were exposed to the workings of the Church, to sermons, to the lofty voices of the choirs, to the hollow beauty of the spaces. You felt a certain measure of comfort and ease inside a church. Did you believe in God?

You believed in something, although I'm not sure you would have called it "God." But music leans into religion. A lot of music was composed in service to the Church, and I think that by virtue of playing it, you were infused with its purpose. One of the last pieces you played, one that you practised through-out your last few months, was Ravel's *Menuet antique*. You said to Mum that you thought of it as a prayer, and that you just wanted to play it over and over again.

Were you made in part by the music that you played? And if so, when you died, the silence we were left with was that same silence that exists in a concert hall the moment after the music stops—a silence that still tastes of the sound it carried.

17

Everything holds memory. A house will remember a person after he's gone by the slight sway in the floorboards in the front room at the window where he used to stand for hours. It remembers the pot of geraniums on the back porch by the faded circle in the grey paint. We move through spaces that have held onto other lives and will learn the shape of ours, will hold onto the way we walk through rooms, how we touch what we touch. Buildings are alive. Land has memory. Water running underground sounds like a woman crying.

Flotsam once meant everything afloat that was not owned. Wrack was the black line on the beach that marked the stranding point for cast-up seaweed and ship's wreckage. A skyscraper was the highest triangular sail on a fully rigged ship. A guzzle was a place where storms had once crossed and might cross again—a low, perhaps damp spot on an estuary or inland from a beach, as far inland sometimes as to be a field, where the sea could enter if it so chose. It is a place that is a ghost, that only exists under certain conditions, when water remembers where it went and what it once touched; when it imagines the shape it once filled and held, when it remembers itself.

In the summer of 1892 August Strindberg tried to photograph the human soul. The soul he tried to photograph was his own with a series of blurry, black and white portraits. In one, he stares out at the camera, eyes dark and defiant, his overcoat undone. He is standing in front of a wooden door. The door rises like a sail behind him as though the weight of this act, the baring of his soul, has sunk him down inside the frame, a human shipwreck.

Everything becomes a memorial. This wooden chair is a memorial to that tree.

The rock is memorial to the mountain. The shadow is memorial to the sun. Everything comes undone. The story is memorial to the experience.

When I swim in the river at the cottage, I swim

over a rock. I know it's large because I first discovered it by banging my foot on it. I know it's not far under the surface. I have learned where it is by lining up objects on the banks to show me its position. When I put my feet upon it I can feel a sharp ridge on top, how the rock rises at one end, drops at the other. Sometimes there are snails attached to it, sometimes weeds. I can describe this rock without ever having seen it—but if I can't see it, then what am I describing?

Something exists more fully as an object when it isn't described. The description is merely another object. The story alters the object. It doesn't experience it.

This space that I write these words down in is the space after the music has left. It is that silence in the concert hall after the last note of the piano has been struck and held and the whispers of that note hush down to nothing, to the emotions left by the music, to the memory of sound.

I think of you sometimes as part of the piano, your body simply an extension of the keys. You must have felt both liberated and oppressed by the fact that the music lived through you, that you were responsible for making it happen, that without your body to animate it there was only silence.

You used to move your hands all the time, your fingers tapping out notes on the tabletop at the bar, or on the legs of your jeans, jammed into your pockets, or smoothing your long hair back. You hummed, and sometimes sang a note straight out, in perfect pitch, to demonstrate a sound or harmonize with another sound. You had played music for so long that, in a sense, you *were* music.

They tied your hands down in the hospital because you kept moving them. They were afraid you'd rip out the ventilator and the PICC line from your neck, and so they restrained you and kept you sedated. And you certainly tried to do these things the nurses were afraid of you doing, but I wonder too if your hands just wanted to move because they were so used to moving over the piano keys. From the age of four, you had played the piano for hours every day and your body still remembered this, even when your mind was juiced up on morphine.

Maybe when you died what left your body, following the last few staccato beats of your racing heart, the last harsh gasping of your breath, was not so much your soul as the last true notes of you.

18

I wasn't where I was supposed to be today. I begged off going to a party at the last minute and went instead for a long walk with the dog. This happens a lot these days; I just can't follow through with all my social obligations. Conversation becomes difficult, and more often than not I simply have nothing to say to other people.

I wanted to find that apple with the pinkish flesh that I had discovered a few weeks ago, so I took Charlotte back through the fields to the tree where the apple had grown. A local gardener had named the apple for me when I described it to her—a Scarlet Pippin—particular to this region of Ontario, this lake country around Kingston, first planted here by settlers in the early 1800s.

The Scarlet Pippin is an early apple that ripens in August and so there was nothing left on the tree when I got there, just a few shrivelled apples lying in the long grass beneath it. I was disappointed, although I don't know why I expected the fruit to still be on the tree. But time has become complicated since you died. Sometimes it collapses entirely, so that a few weeks take on the shape and texture of a single day, and sometimes an hour stretches out as an endless plain before me and I cannot see to the other side of it. I can't seem to negotiate time as well as I did before. It just seems to happen to me, like an accident.

The Scarlet Pippin wasn't there, but when I looked down the field I saw another apple tree, laden with fruit, and beyond that and to the right, another tree. There were three other apple trees in that field, the remains, clearly, of an old orchard. Each tree grew a different variety of apple. I picked samples from the three trees and carried them home in my sweater, so that I could identify them. But before that, I stood in the long grass and ate one apple from each of the three trees. One was sweet, one tart, and one had an oblong shape with hard, white flesh. In apple terminology, an oblong shape is called *oblate*.

I have become a little obsessed with apples since

you died, with the small orchard that I'm trying to grow at the cottage. I'm not sure why exactly, but I've learned not to question anything these days. Like a child, or an animal perhaps, I simply move towards what feels good and move away from what feels bad. Taking care of the fruit trees at the cottage feels right, and so I put my limited energies and focus there.

My orchard is still too young to properly produce, and the trees that have shown the most promise are the pears and the cherries, but it is the apples that have my attention. It is the apples I gravitate towards.

I like that apple trees are all individuals, that no two trees are alike, and even if a seed from one apple is planted, the tree that grows from that seed will not have exactly the same apples as the first tree. It is endlessly possible to make new varieties of apples by grafting one variety onto the rootstock of another, or even by grafting one variety onto a branch of another, so that the branch will grow one type of apple and the rest of the tree will grow another.

I like that there are all these old lost orchards in southern Ontario. Sometimes there is only a single tree remaining, and sometimes, as here, there are several trees, each growing a different variety of apple. I can graft pieces of the old trees onto my new trees and, in that way, preserve some of the old species, even though the new apples that grow will not be completely the same as the old.

But grafting is about bringing something back, keeping something alive, moving the essence of something from one place to another, from one *body* to another.

Down the river from my cottage, out past habitation, in the wild part that resembles the everglades, a single apple tree hangs over the water. It produces a fruit that is related to a Snow apple at the end of September. The field behind the tree is a tangle of bushes and brambles, with no sign of a building, and yet once there must have been an old farmhouse there, someone must have planted that apple tree with other apple trees, and those trees would have been part of the fruit source for that family. Early apples for eating. Late apples for cider and sauce.

The spring after you died I took a couple of grafting courses, because I want to wander out in the world and find these old trees, bring pieces of them back to my young orchard and grow new fruit that tastes of the old fruit.

I like the laws of grafting:

When planting a whip grafted onto rootstock, always bury the graft so that the new tree doesn't have to spend energy trying to protect it.

Protect the graft because it is vulnerable. New growth is vulnerable, and will burn or freeze first.

Never graft into a colder season.

An orchard is an assembly, a community. The trees produce fruit at different times, but they are united in their common purpose, and they rely on one another. Many fruit trees require others of their species for cross-pollination. In this way, perhaps, an orchard is a conversation among the various trees. The trees, although single entities, are always in relation to one another. A conversation. A family.

There's a choreography to an orchard. Over time, some of the trees in an orchard will have died due to disease or age, and new ones will have been planted in their place. Or, the orchardist might have removed certain trees in favour of other ones that are more suited to growing there. The family of a friend had a peach orchard in Niagara for generations, but they ripped it out in favour of planting cherry trees because they could make more money from running a pick-your-own cherry orchard than they could from selling peaches.

An orchard is a society, but an orchard is also a place—a temple, an orchestrated wildness, a space made by humans that doesn't look human. The way an orchard is planted and re-planted becomes a conversation, not just among the trees, but across the generations of people who tend the orchard. The new owners of an orchard act in response to the decisions made by former owners. Orchards are always full of wildlife. The fruit attracts birds and insects and squirrels, raccoons and deer. An orchard offers itself equally to the air and to the earth.

The grandfather we never knew, Dad's father, who died in the war, shot down in a Wellington bomber over the Mediterranean one March night on his way to take control of an airbase in Malta at the age of forty-five (the same age you were when you died)—he always wanted to have an orchard. He had been called out of retirement to fly this one last mission, but his plan for after the war ended was to move his family to Trail, British Columbia, and start a fruit farm.

It was a strange dream for an Englishman, but he had spent a few years in his early twenties in Vancouver and Victoria, and maybe he had travelled outside the cities and seen the orchards then, and the impression of them had remained with him, through both world wars and through his time in Singapore and England. I sometimes wonder if any of the trees I am planting in my small orchard are trees that he would have planted in his, if we are having a conversation this way, across the years, across death itself.

There's an old orchard I see when I drive the highway back and forth between Kingston and Toronto. The trees are huge, in need of pruning, clearly not tended, but still producing prolifically. When it's apple season the orchard is filled with horses from the neighbouring farm, contentedly eating the fallen fruit.

I like that orchards are planted for food, not decoration, as gardens are, that their reason for being is human hunger and their success or failure is tied to that hunger, and since hunger is tied to desire, there is something of the erotic in an orchard, something of desire itself. It's not hard to see how the story of Adam and Eve and the forbidden fruit originated.

Right after you died I tried to write, but there seemed nothing to say. But I've been a writer all my life and, like the muscle memory in an athlete, my writing memory is hard to stop, even when the motivation is gone. I had nothing to say, no story to tell, but I needed to write, and so I worked for a couple of hours every morning simply copying out the salient details from an encyclopedia of apples published in 1905.

I didn't get very far with my apple notations, only to the Arthur apple, but the routine helped. It's how I've always taught myself something, to start at the beginning and just keep going through to the end, systematically. When I graduated from high school, instead of attending university I went to the local library and started reading from *A* in the Literature section. That took longer than I'd bargained for and I only got to *M* before skipping ahead to *W* so that I could read the novels and diaries of Virginia Woolf.

So I wrote down the descriptions of the apples from the encyclopedia, and often, interspersed with the descriptions, I wrote down what I could of how I was feeling. When I look through the notebook now, it's a jumble of things: *Allison—valuable winter apple from Tennessee—oblate, rather strongly ribbed, sides unequal, rather uniform—heavily splashed with large and small russet patches—nearly sweet—late winter.* And that description followed by: *Grief enjoys shorthand, that's what I'm thinking today. Narrative is too fluid. Grief is all chop, all rhythm and breaks, broken. It is the lurch of the heart, not the steady beating of it.*

I turn to that same apple catalogue to identify the three trees in the old orchard that I found today. Baldwin. Tolman Sweet. Yellow Pearmain.

19

I'm on a train, riding through the flat southwestern Ontario landscape in the early morning. The sun isn't up yet, but the horizon is tinged pink with the promise of it. The clouds are low, dark streaks over the fields.

There was a beautiful sunrise on the December morning that you died. I woke early in your new apartment that day and just lay there in the dark for a while before getting up. Mum had arrived by then and I had given her your bed. I slept on the divan in the living room, in a sort of propped-up position that was not as uncomfortable as it had seemed it might be. Sleeping in the front room was noisy because Hastings Street was right outside the window and there was always traffic moving up and down it, day or night. I liked waking early in your apartment and lying in the dark looking at your books in the bookcases, your pictures stacked against the walls. Your possessions were comforting, familiar. I had woken to these same objects many times over the years, in all of the places you had lived.

After you died, when I was coming back to your apartment to clean it out, I was looking forward to seeing your space with your things as you had arranged them. But there had been an infestation of bedbugs in your building in my absence, and your landlady had sprayed your apartment, and to do that she'd had to move everything away from the walls, so that your stuff was just a piled jumble in the centre of each room. All the careful placement of your items, that delicate arrangement, gone.

The sunrise was visible from the hospital corridor windows on the walk to your room in the ICU. I remember stopping at the windows for a moment before continuing in to see you, and just watching the deep red of the sky. That afternoon, after you died, the sky was the same colour over the mountains on the way out of the hospital. It almost felt as if time hadn't advanced at all, that the hours between the sunrise and sunset had never happened.

When I stood at the window that morning, watching the sunrise, I knew that you were going to die that day. The doctor had said to us the afternoon before, "We need to think about letting him go."

This sunrise isn't quite as good as that one. Maybe the cold air over the mountains helped to stain the sky such a dark red that morning. Here, the space above the fields is infused with pink, a smudge of colour over the dark trees.

I'm on my way back from a reading. The book we went to Paris to research is finally out and I've been travelling around to promote it. Maybe you would like it, Martin. I'm not sure, because you never read my books. I don't know why. You kept all my reviews, though. I found them after you died. I asked you several times why you didn't read my books, but you never gave me a real answer. In the last few months you did make an effort to right this, by starting one of my novels, but you only got to page 54.

My novel was by your bed in your Vancouver apartment when I got there. I guess you were still trying to read it. The objects in the orbit of a bed are the objects most in use, and that was certainly the case with you. The space around your bed was strewn with books, papers, your cell phone and charger, clothes, a glass of water. Everything you needed, every night, close at hand.

I used to be upset that you didn't read my books, but it no longer matters. I understand that it cost you to be a child prodigy, that starting piano so young and having an art that was public meant that for years, you felt people only liked you for your music, and not for yourself.

Two women are sitting behind me on the train. They've been talking the whole time, crazy talk. "I used to have a lot of friends before my head injury," one of them says. The other one counters with, "Do you know what the leading cause of death for women in Canada is? Urinary tract infections." I love every crazy sentence that comes out of their mouths. I love their absolute belief that they're being ripped off, and that everything that happens to them is someone else's fault.

The sun is up now, Martin, and the fields are gold and green, and the trees mass green at the edges, and the train lurches forward, and the sunrise has evaporated, and this day is fully underway.

20

You were practising three piano pieces during the fall you were dying. The first was the *Menuet antique* by Ravel, the piece you told Mum was like a prayer.

The *Menuet* was the first of Ravel's compositions to be published. It was a piece written in youth, when he was twenty years old. Like you, Ravel was an owl rather than a lark, preferring to work at night, and often taking long walks in the dark. He liked the darkness so much that he had the shapes of stars cut into the wooden shutters in his house, so he could imagine the night sky during the daylight hours.

Music was his only intimate and he never married or, apparently, had lovers. He embraced the loneliness of being an artist, or fell into it so far that he couldn't climb back out again. It always amuses me when people refer to this way of living as a "choice" because it certainly doesn't feel that way. To turn towards creative work is, by necessity, to turn away from human society. It is not really a choice; the drive to do this, the pull, comes from somewhere outside oneself. I feel this, and I know that you did too. And clearly Ravel, for all of his sixty-two years on earth, felt it as well.

Debussy's *Suite bergamasque* was written from the poems of Paul Verlaine. The famous third movement of the piece, called "Clair de Lune" (Moonlight) was taken from the following poem, written in 1869, which I know you have read:

Your soul is a select landscape
Where charming masqueraders and bergamaskers go
Playing the lute and dancing and almost
Sad beneath their fantastic disguises.

All sing in a minor key
Of victorious love and the opportune life,
They do not seem to believe in their happiness
And their song mingles with the moonlight,

With the still moonlight, sad and beautiful,
That sets the birds dreaming in the trees
And the fountains sobbing in ecstasy,
The tall slender fountains among marble statues.

Debussy wanted his music to be an emotional experience, to be about the emotions, and this is what you wanted too. You said to me, more than once, that you were tired of people going about their day trying not to feel, being afraid of emotion, and that what you wanted your music to do was simply make people feel something.

Fauré's *Theme and Variations* is sombre, and even though the piece leaves that shadowy place and escapes into one variation after another, it always returns to that darkness. It is not hard to see why you chose to play it, why you chose to let it speak for you.

These were the pieces that kept you company that last fall, that you gave your failing strength to, and that you tried to perfect. This is where you put the knowledge of your impending death. This is what you gave yourself over to, and what held you up during those final few months.

It wasn't bad company to keep.

At the end, in the hospital, we borrowed a CD

player from the nurses' station so that we could have music playing for you while you lay sedated and hooked up to the ventilator. Your friends brought in CDs that they thought you'd like, and every morning Cathy and I took a couple of CDs from the collection in your apartment. We rotated through them. The music played day and night in your room, most of it piano music. All three of the pieces that you had been learning to play that fall were there, performed by different pianists, none of them, frankly, sounding as good as you.

We thought the music would be a comfort to you, but I wonder now if it wasn't a torture instead. The sound would have let you know that people were in the room with you. Sometimes we'd put on a particular CD and you'd thrash your head around as though you were trying to communicate something, although it was impossible to know what that might be. Either one of two things, I guess—that you liked the music, or that you wanted us to turn it off.

21

Your two CDs were reissued after you died. Now Mum and Dad are at work putting out your live recordings. There will be three discs, released in chronological order. The first one will be ready in a week or two. This would please you, I think. The first disc is solo piano and has you playing Chopin, Ravel, and your own composition, "Winterscapes."

When you were first diagnosed and I went to your house in Toronto to see you, we went for a walk around the block. We laughed about your prognosis because it seemed so unbelievable. *I don't want to die,* you said. "But you're not dead yet," I said. Nobody knew then how shockingly fast it would all go. Now I drive by your old neighbourhood often, right past those streets where we walked. If I look quickly, out of the corner of my eye, I can almost see us there. You, stopping to light a cigarette. Me, bending down to pat a dog.

On that visit, you gave me two file boxes to take away with me to our parents' house, which, in your panicked state, you suddenly thought would be a safer place to keep them than at your own house. One box contained your compositions, and the other was filled with recordings of your live performances. *Guard them with your life,* you said—because they *were* your life, all the meat of your years in those two boxes that I could lift together and place in the trunk of my car.

You were always trying to compose, but there was never enough time. Your ideas and the notes for your ideas carried over from year to year, with little or no advancement. "Winterscapes," which will be on that first live CD, was written more than ten years ago, when, miraculously, you had a few days in Montreal and could sit and watch the snow fall outside your window and were moved to write a piece about that. But you still had plans to rewrite it. This was on your list of *Things To Do Before I Die.*

"Winterscapes" was about the loneliness of winter. In your introduction to the piece when you performed it, you said it was about *somebody sitting by a window and looking outside, and becoming quite entranced by what they see, which causes them to look inward.*

You made your living teaching and accompanying and examining, all work that was done piecemeal, so that you were constantly stringing together your part-time jobs, and eventually this meant that you worked all the time. There was no day off in a week. There was no time to reflect, gather your thoughts, write down a phrase, and then another. There was no time to compose, which was what I'm sure you would say you really wanted to do.

But you were a good teacher, a natural one. After you died, cards came in from so many of your current and former students, all of them saying how encouraging and supportive you were, how patient and kind, what generosity of spirit you had.

One former student wrote, "I credit Martin for my success in piano, but more importantly, my enjoyment in playing the piano. During the many years of piano lessons, Martin was not simply my piano teacher, but he was also my friend."

Your own notes on music were both direct and comprehensive. You advised that *Thinking of where you want to clear the pedal (instead of put the pedal down) often works well.* And you offered the simple thought,

If you're having trouble with the fingering, think of the music. You dismissed various "methods" for playing the piano—high wrists, low wrists, curved fingers, flat fingers—saying that *music is far too varied to have one solution.* Of Rachmaninoff's *Variations* you wrote, *This builds, but also changes gradually (is it necessary to produce the sense of building, or is it better to play each variation to the utmost of its character?).* For the first movement of Beethoven's *Moonlight Sonata* you decided that the *entire movement keeps shifting back to minor chords, therefore do not make the major chords too bright.*

A lot of the composers you admired, and the writers I admired, had functioned, in their time, without much money. They lived in drafty apartments, nursed one coffee all afternoon while writing in a café because it was warmer than where they lived. They were inspired to create, but underneath that was always the struggle to earn enough money to pay the rent, to get by. You and I were no different in that respect. It's always been hard to earn a living, and sometimes it's been brutal. It surprised me, when I became a writer, to discover that many writers these days come from money, have an independent income, or are supported by someone else.

But that was never the case for you or me. And

for you perhaps it was harder because the nature of your work meant that you were required to work day and night. I remember trying to make a date to meet you for a beer when you were back in Toronto, and the only time you had free to meet, when you would have a couple of hours to spare, was Sunday night at 10 p.m.

In the list of what you wanted to work on, written down in a red hardcover notebook that you kept with you all through that last fall, you had this: *Cello Sonata, Musical, Dance for Two, Pieces in Montreal—for starters, then a lot more things.*

The "Cello Sonata" is little more than a few bars, written in your trademark light pencil markings, in your composition notebook. "Dance for Two" is really the only completed piece of music, and I know you would have kept tinkering with it, but we have had to count it as finished. Your friend Bernie, and Mum, worked from the almost impossible-to-read manuscript and transcribed a final version. We had the first two bars carved onto your tombstone.

"Dance for Two" was the only finished piece for your musical. You said to me, more than once, that you thought the musical was the most perfect art form. You were excited to be writing one. Initially, you had asked me to collaborate with you. We had always talked of working together one day, but we also thought there would be more time, that we could just keep putting off that day because it would still be there when we wanted it to be.

When you went into the hospital in Toronto for a couple of days at the end of September, that first time, for a bowel blockage that needed hydration and morphine to fix it, you asked me to work on the musical with you. The morphine, and the relief from the pain, had put you in a good mood. You were happy, full of creative spirit. You had been writing poems about the dawn each day at the hospital, and making notes about your musical. "Okay," I said. I already knew the story of the musical because you'd told it to me numerous times. "I'll write the words for you."

Oh, but I want to do the words, you said. And we laughed, because although it seemed like a good idea to work together, in reality you didn't want to give up any control over your project.

I thought later about what you said, Martin, about the musical being a perfect art form. I can see what you mean, although I would choose a sonnet over a musical as the perfect form. A musical is all plot points, each song detailing a specific decisive moment in the narrative, or relaying key information. There is no nuance, no description, all the atmosphere is done with props. It's character and feeling, how we tell stories to one another—"this happened, and then this happened next."

Your musical was going to have two acts. The main story was of a developer and a politician who were in league to exploit a town and its citizens. The developer owned a factory where the male lead (Jack) worked. There were safety issues at the factory and at the end of the first act Jack loses his life on the job, and returns in the second act as a ghost. He is in love with a young woman (whose name keeps changing in the notes you made). Jack comes back to her as a ghost, but she can't see him. She lobbies against the politician and developer because of Jack's death, and she is able to stop their corrupt plans for the town.

You had names for almost everyone, and ideas for their songs. Adam is the developer. Trixie is his girlfriend. She is a hairdresser. You were going to have a scene in the hair salon with a chorus of women sitting in chairs, singing, *Trixie, Trixie, will you cut my hair* ...

The politician is named Tim, and he is backed by a chorus of men, thugs, known as the Morrissey Boys. There's a doctor, simply called "Doc." She's there to preside over Jack's death, but you had no songs sketched out for her yet. When she first appears on stage, she asks the audience how they are feeling.

You had most of Adam's solo worked out by the time I came to see you in hospital that first time. You sang me the tune, with the lyrics, snapping your fingers to the beat. *I am Adam. / Get down on your knees. / I am Adam. / I do what I please.*

"Dance for Two" is a song without words. It opens the second act, or closes the first one. I can't remember now what you wanted. But I do know that the dance is performed by Jack's lover outside, at night. You imagined that the dance would take place on a bluff overlooking the moonlit water below. But that would have been hard to stage, and I think that was just a slippage from childhood. We grew up near the bluffs in Scarborough. We often rode our bikes to the bluffs when we were children, or sat on the edge of them as teenagers, smoking and drinking. You walked back to them a few times when you were ill and staying at our parents' house. They were always compelling: that strict three-hundred-foot drop to the lake, the crumbling sandstone cliffs. Once, as children, we dared our wildest friend to ride his bike off the bluffs. He began pedalling in the middle of the park towards the drop, and I remember his hurtling flight across the grass, how his bike soared, spectacularly, right out past the edge, hung in the air for a moment and then dropped straight down. He snagged on some tree roots about sixty feet below and had to be rescued by the fire department. His bike was a tangled twist of metal at the bottom of the cliffs.

I think that you were Jack. When you told me that your main character was going to die after the first act, I said, "Well, then, how can you have a second act without him?"

I know, you said. *It's a problem. But he has to die.*

It's what you hoped, I suppose, what we all hoped—that somehow you would come back as a ghost, that you would find your way home.

You wrote a song for your female lead to sing after her lover died. In all your other notes for the musical, you interspersed words and music, notes dashed down and words scrawled on top of them. But in this song there are only words, and they are written out neatly, in stanzas, like a poem.

Jack, where are you—where have you—where have you gone?
I'm inside of you, and you're inside of me.
But where have we—where have we gone?
Where are we now?

22

I remember you being born. It was the end of May and there was a heat wave. I was wearing shorts because my legs were sticking to the orange plastic chair in the hospital waiting room. Also, my legs didn't touch the floor, because I remember the feel of swinging them back and forth as Dad and I waited for Mum to come downstairs with the new baby.

I had wished and wished for a baby brother, and so it felt as though the fact of it coming true had something to do with that wish. I could hardly wait to see you for the first time. You were wrapped tightly in a blue blanket (everything was strictly gender colour-coded in those days). You didn't cry. I was allowed to hold you all the way home in the taxi, and I was careful not to move in case I made you upset.

I adored you as my little brother, and later Cathy adored you as her big brother. Our parents cherished you as their only son, and later they worshipped you for your musical gifts. From winning piano competitions when you were a child, to finishing your ARCT when you were thirteen, to debuting at the Royal Festival Hall in England at twenty, you were always revered for your musical ability.

You were born into this atmosphere of utter adoration, which at first you took for granted, and later craved but did not trust.

There was a period when you rebelled against the piano because you felt that everyone only liked you for your talent, not for your real self. You struggled with these feelings for years. I asked you in the fall that you were dying if you still felt conflicted. *I've made peace with it,* you said. *I love the piano.*

I think that you, like me, had done the same thing so intensely, and for so long, that it was impossible to know where it ended and you began. The piano, once "other," was now you, and it could be relied upon to express your feelings rather than to simply absorb them.

23

I loved that you chose as your bank code the first
four notes of Beethoven's Fifth Symphony—5552.

24

You can fall into music, and maybe music is better company than writing because it makes a sound, takes up human space, a dimension in the world. It releases emotion, whereas writing pins emotion down. And all writing is necessarily elegiac because it happens after the moment it seeks to capture.

25

There's a frost out this morning. The first frost this fall, and the crisp of the ground and the cold of the air makes me think of you, of your dying season, and how we've entered it once again.

The dog's breath came in clouds as she tore through the fields this morning. The heat of her, in the cold mouth of the day.

What I was thinking today was how when we were children there was that big climbing frame in the backyard. We spent a lot of time on it, scaling the ladders up the sides, hanging upside down from the bars at the top. It was elaborate and compli-cated and had taken our parents a full weekend to assemble. Each of the bars was a different colour—

blue, red, yellow, silver—although the silver ones eventually rusted out and our clothes were always smudged with that orange dust.

We were the only ones on the street who had a climbing frame and so our yard was often filled with other children. One day, we were all on the frame, about seven of us, and you fell off. Remember, Martin? Your teeth went straight through your tongue and there was a great gush of blood. Your tongue was partially severed and it took numerous stitches to close the wound, all without anesthetic. But before that—before the drive to the emergency department, before I even screamed for Mum—when you were crouched on the grass, bleeding, I chased everyone else out of the yard. I was convinced that someone had pushed you, and since I didn't know who it was, I just got rid of them all.

What I was thinking this morning was how this wasn't much different from the way I behaved at the hospital in Burnaby at the end of your life. I made rules of conduct for your bedside. No one was allowed to cry, or talk over your prone body as though you weren't there. No one was allowed to tell you that you were dying, or make references to your death. All the talk had to be positive, because all you knew was that you had come to the hospital for an emergency operation, and that you had survived the operation. You didn't know anything beyond that. I'm still convinced this was true. You didn't know you were dying, and when you were dead, you didn't know that you were dead.

But I think you know now.

I wanted to protect you, as always. I wanted you to be able to have your own feelings, whatever they were, and not be burdened with the sorrows and tears of everyone else—because you were a natural empathizer and would have found it easier to take on other people's feelings than to acknowledge or struggle with your own.

Right or wrong, I would do it all again.

I would chase everyone out of that yard.

26

This is what I saw when I was out with the dog: a monarch butterfly, lifting above the milkweed in the October field. Between the feet of the butterfly, its wings closed up so that it was being carried by the tips of its wings, was a dead butterfly, another monarch. My initial thought was that the first butterfly was going to eat the second, was taking it somewhere for that purpose. My next thought was that they knew each other, that the living butterfly was a familiar of the dead butterfly and could not leave it, could not abandon it to death.

The flight was difficult. The weight of the dead butterfly slowed the momentum of the living one, kept it barely airborne, but it struggled on regardless, would not relinquish its burden.

The mechanics of your death were simple. Your blood pressure dropped, and your heart raced, faster and faster, trying to pump blood through your leaking blood vessels. The flutter of your heart in your chest was exactly like the flutter of this butterfly's wings as it tried to keep aloft.

27

I wrote your obituary on the plane home from Vancouver, on the morning of December fourth. I sat with a notebook and pen, in a middle seat, on a big Airbus, and tried to reduce your spirit to a series of adjectives, your life to a list of accomplishments. I wrote and cried and no one talked to me. I think I gave off such a stench of grief that the people on either side of me just kept their heads down in their books.

It was easy to know what to say first: *concert pianist.* You had worked your whole life for that. It was pretty much your molecular structure.

The list of accomplishments came effortlessly, and even the order seemed to be the right order.

*Concert pianist, teacher, composer, accompanist, Royal
Conservatory examiner, son, brother, beloved friend.*

It was harder knowing what to write about your
self. I wanted to be honest, not just focus on your
good qualities but include some of your more difficult aspects. Because, like everyone, you were complicated, and sometimes your traits did double duty.
Your stubbornness, for example, could be obstinacy
or it could be determination.

Death makes a small story of life because suddenly there's an end to it, and it can be summed
up. Someone can be reduced to a handful of words.
I don't know what you would think of the words I
used to describe your life, but know that I am in the
business of choosing words carefully, and I never
chose words more carefully than the ones I selected
for your obituary.

*Brilliant, talented, passionate and compassionate,
kind, handsome, disciplined, elusive, and stubborn,
Martin loved music, art, new places and experiences,
his friends, the West Coast, connecting with life in all
its forms, having a beer, and watching the Maple Leafs
(even this season). He hated cruelty, intolerance, stupid-
ity, and Toronto winters.*

*He died too soon, from pancreatic cancer, and is
deeply missed by his parents, Frances and Anthony; his*

sisters, Helen and Cathy; his many friends in Vancouver, Toronto, England, and Paris. We are lost without his beautiful spirit.

28

Most of the patients in the ICU were elderly. You shared your room with a woman in her seventies who had had a stroke. She moaned a lot and flailed around. She was on a ventilator for the first few days, but by the end she was off that and talking in a raspy voice to her family. Her bed was by the window, where I wished yours could have been because you would have been able to feel the sunlight.

I grew to resent that old woman, because of the noise she made, and because she recovered. Every day she became a little better, and every day you became a little worse. In fact, all the elderly patients on the ward were going to get better, and only you and another young man were going to die. That man, who was around the same age as you, had had a stroke deep in the centre of his brain and he was bleeding out into his brain. The bleed was inoperable and would eventually shut down his cognitive functions. His girlfriend would have to make the decision to take him off life support, just a few days after we would make that decision for you.

We saw that family every day in the little waiting area outside the ICU where they made us come before we could be admitted to your room. The room had about ten seats in it, and a TV mounted on one wall. A couple of small side tables were piled with out-of-date magazines. The walls of the room were that institutional beige that is so unpleasant to look at if you are forced to spend large amounts of time doing just that.

On one of the side tables was a phone. When we arrived at the waiting room we were to call through to the nurses' station, and say who we were and who we wanted to see, and then they would decide whether or not we could be admitted. This process made me nervous. I was afraid sometimes that you had disappeared in the night, or that I wouldn't be allowed in to see you. But although I was often made to wait, it was only because your dressings were being changed, and the nurses were always apologetic about the delay.

The man with the stroke had been sent to ICU around the same time as you, so we were with his family for the duration of those ten days you were in hospital. He had a complicated family. His girlfriend was new, and young. He also had a wife, from whom he was separated but not divorced, and children. There was clearly animosity between these two groups of people, and they tried not to overlap at the hospital. If they did happen to overlap, there was often shouting and finger-pointing between the wife and the girlfriend.

But mostly this didn't happen. Mostly they came separately, and the girlfriend was there every day, the wife less frequently.

The girlfriend came with her mother, and we all sat there—us on one side of the room, and them on the other; the space between our two families so little that if there had been a table in that space, we would all be sitting around it.

I liked seeing them every day. Sometimes we said a few words to one another. Mostly we just smiled and nodded. Often one or the other of us was crying, and we would look away in that small room, to give the crying person some privacy. When you died, and we were leaving the hospital, the mother rushed after us to say that she was sorry and to hug us goodbye.

Unexpectedly, we had a lot of company in that place of fear and grief. There were those families in the waiting room who were suffering through the same ordeal. There were the doctors and nurses, particularly the nurses, who were with you every day, sitting in the room with you, changing your dressings, monitoring your vital signs. The nurses were amazing, and you would have especially liked the nurse who had the same name as one of your old girlfriends, and who came back on her night off just to check on how you were doing after you'd had to have the second emergency bowel surgery.

You would also have liked the anesthetist, who came to talk to us when Mum and Dad were at the hospital, to say how sorry he was that you had died. I asked him if you had been afraid, and he said that you just told him to make sure you didn't feel any pain. But clearly you had had a conversation with him, and I'm sure, knowing you, that the conversation was also about him in some way. That is why he had remembered you. He was impressed enough by that encounter to want to share with us your last fully conscious moments.

The surgeon who performed the second emergency operation took the time to reassure me that your cancer was a complete fluke, that it wasn't a result of genetics or lifestyle. It had simply happened, without explanation or cause.

Now, when people are afraid of entering that death tunnel, whether it is their own impending death or that of someone close to them, I tell them that although it may be devastating, they won't be alone. They will have good company—people who, while they may not know the individual who is dying, will fully understand the situation. This, in itself, is immensely comforting. In this place where you feel nothing but alone, you are not alone. And it makes a difference. It makes the unbearable less so.

29

This is a story I always wanted to tell you, to write
to you, but I never did. It is a story of the last time I
was in Italy, when I went to visit Keats's apartment
in Rome. It is a story about dying, one that would
have appealed to your romantic imagination, and a
story that might have given you a measure of comfort.

So, I'll tell it to you now.

It is a long climb up the stairs to number 26 the
Piazza di Spagna, to the two small rooms and the
tiny terrace let to John Keats in the summer of
1820.

This is the room where Keats died at the age of
twenty-five. There is a narrow bed and a view out the

window of the Spanish Steps. In the room there are white daisies embossed on the pale blue ceiling, a marble fireplace. When Keats was in this room there would have been the easel and brushes of his friend, the artist Joseph Severn, and perhaps vases bristling with flowers, the smell of coffee, the sound of church bells.

At the bottom of the Spanish Steps is a marble fountain in the shape of a sinking boat. The middle of the boat is filled with water, the two broken ends sticking out from the pool almost at right angles as if the boat has snapped amidships. As the day begins and the people of Rome start to move the city from slumber, it seems that the men and women climbing the long flight up from the fountain to the church at the top of the steps are ascending out of the wreckage, walking up from the water and the ruined boat, towards salvation.

When Keats came to Rome in 1820 with his friend Joseph Severn, he felt he was already dead because his great love, Fanny Brawne, had refused his offer of marriage. He believed it would be too painful to continue contact with her while he lay dying, so forbade her to write or visit him. "I have already died," he said when he left England and the love of Fanny Brawne. Those final weeks in Rome were what he called his "posthumous life."

After Keats died, the rooms and furniture were scrubbed down to erase any lingering traces of the TB that had killed him. Now his death mask stands by the bed, a lock of his wheaten hair under glass nearby. There's a page in his own hand, also under glass, miraculous in its intactness because Severn destroyed a lot of Keats's poetry and letters by cutting individual lines out to send to the women who wrote begging for something in his handwriting.

From where Keats lay in his bed he would have looked out the window and seen nothing but sky, a small, blue box of sky. The colour might have changed very slowly, as the sky held light or leaked it. The wind might sometimes have rattled the window.

The Spanish Steps were constructed by Francesco de Sanctis in 1723 to 1725. They were intended to broach the steep Pincian Hill and to connect the lower Piazza di Spagna with the upper Piazza di Trinita dei Monti. They were designed on a theatrical scale, with a straight flight of steps flanked by a pair of convex staircases. The design includes broad landings and a series of curving flights. One can climb straight up via the central staircase, or proceed in a slow, winding promenade to the top, stopping along the way to lean over the balcony railing and gaze down at the fountain below. The staircase is believed to be based on the sweeping moves of a dance—the Polonaise.

The Spanish Steps are crowded on summer nights with people moving up and down the staircase that echoes the dance. Below the human noises there is the shuffle of the fountain as the boat sinks and sinks, and the water empties from between its bones.

Keats could not bear to be read to while he was on his deathbed. He did not believe in the comfort of religion, nor did he believe in life after death. He did entertain, sometimes, the romantic fantasy that life was the dream and that death would be the awakening from that dream.

Keats knew that there is an undeniable lyric truth to life. This is to be found in nature, in gesture, in love. He knew this when he tried to match his line of poetry to the bend of the river grasses, or the song of the nightingale.

In that room where there was no writing and no reading, Severn sketched the dying man, in fact made some of the finest drawings of the poet when he was on his deathbed. Perhaps Severn's sketching was a comforting presence to Keats. Art, although no longer of urgent relevance to his world, would have been his familiar.

Severn, afraid that he'd fall asleep one night and that Keats would wake to darkness and think that he had died, devised a system so that the poet would have continuous light. He fastened a piece of thread from the bottom of one candle to the wick of another, and in its guttering state the dying flame would ignite the thread and travel up it to ignite the wick of the next candle.

It is said that John Keats awoke at the exact moment the flame was travelling up the thread from one candle to another, and that in his excitement at witnessing this spectacle, he woke Severn to tell him of the success of his invention.

At the end, we are all far from home. We are far from home, and what we hope for is that someone will fashion us a light, so that we too will not have to wake in darkness.

30

When I look back at your dying, I am still astonished by how quickly everything moved, how much of a scramble it was to adjust to the rapid and unrecoverable changes.

At the end of July you were diagnosed with inoperable pancreatic cancer, stage 4B, the cancer having metastasized into your liver. Your symptoms prior to this had been a backache and some acid reflux when eating. The first doctor you went to see prescribed muscle relaxants for you, never thinking to send you for a CAT scan because you were so healthy. By the time you went to see the second doctor, everyone had convinced you that you probably had an ulcer, since you had had one when you were a child and your stomach still sometimes bothered you when you ate.

At the beginning of September you started chemo, in hopes it would shrink the tumour on the pancreas and take away some of the pain, and extend your life by a few months. Your initial diagnosis had been death in three to six months, but there was a possibility that you could survive a year or two.

At the end of September you went into hospital in Toronto for a weekend to treat a bowel blockage. You were dosed with morphine to unclench the bowel, and rehydrated because you kept refusing to drink any water and were always suffering from dehydration.

At the end of October, when you had a bit of a reprieve and weren't feeling quite so ill, we went to New York for a few days.

At the beginning of November, after the first round of chemo had ended, you moved back to Vancouver. On November twenty-second you went into hospital. On December third you died. On December tenth you were buried.

At each stage you struggled to keep up with the changes the disease was causing, and we struggled to keep up with you. The ground was always slippery. Sometimes things would remain the same for a few days, but then they shifted again, and again, and the landscape became completely unfamiliar. You said to me once that the cancer felt like a wild animal was eating you from the inside.

The doctors who treated you also used metaphors to describe what was happening, and it made me realize that they had fashioned these metaphors to avoid having to say anything directly, probably to avoid feeling their patients' raw pain. A metaphor is once removed from the experience. It's safer. It's a story, an image, something to focus on to avoid thinking about what it really means.

The doctor who gave you the initial diagnosis, after the first CAT scan, said, "The horse is already out of the barn." You said, *What exactly does that mean?* and he just repeated the phrase to you, instead of having the courage to say, "You're dying. There is no hope. You probably only have a few months. You can do chemo to reduce the symptoms, but it will not change the prognosis." He did say, "You should probably get your affairs in order."

The pain doctor at the hospital where you went at the end of September said that there was a big difference between dying when elderly and dying in the middle of life. When you're old there is a natural winnowing of life in preparation for the end, a slowing down. "But when you die in the middle of life," she said, "it's like a train going off the track at full speed. You don't know how to slow down."

The ICU doctor at the hospital where you died had a metaphor that I could tell he was very proud of, a uniquely Canadian metaphor. Sitting on the edge of the conference table where he had gathered us to talk about your condition, he mimed a canoe stroke.

"We're all in the canoe together," he said at the beginning, "and we're holding our own against the current, even though we're fighting our way upstream."

At the end he said, "The current's just too strong. We need to think about letting him go."

After you were dead, from the corridor I saw the doctor through his office window, miming the canoe stroke for another rudderless family.

31

When you were in hospital for the first time, at the end of September, you were happy. The pain you'd been feeling from the bowel blockage was eased by the morphine. Your dehydration was cured with a fluid drip. You had a private room with a whole wall of windows and your own bathroom. *I could live in here,* you said when I came to visit. I knew what you meant, that all you'd ever really wanted was a small, clean, bright, orderly space in which to create.

The hospital was perched on the edge of a valley and the windows overlooked the tops of the trees and the wide swath of green that continued over to the opposite ridge. We couldn't see the river at the bottom of the valley from the windows, but I knew that it was there because we'd played in that place when we were children. The river was where we had swum and caught fish, where your Queen's Jubilee towel got swept away during the flooding after a rainstorm.

You kept the blinds fully open, night and day, and you awoke each morning at dawn, and for each of the two days that you were in that hospital, you wrote a poem about the sun coming up.

You had not written poems before, had not undertaken any art form aside from composing for and playing the piano. But there was no piano for you to play at the hospital, and I think that creativity was a force in you that had to be satisfied, and that while you were lying on your back in a hospital bed, writing a poem about the dawn was something manageable.

I am no different. I once went to an arts colony for a month to finish a novel and abandoned the novel the second day I was there. The live-in studio I had been given, in the middle of the woods, had a piano in it because the space was meant for composers as well as writers.

All around me, in all the other cabins spread out over the 450 acres of the arts colony, artists were happily industrious. At dinner people were abuzz with their own genius and productivity. There were endless stories of endless brilliant ideas and I was soon sick of all of them.

I didn't do any writing, but I was seized by a sort of rogue creativity, the spirit of the place perhaps, where artists had been coming to paint and sculpt and compose for a hundred and fifty years. I didn't write, but I started to play the piano in my studio, even though I hadn't played since I was seven years old. I made up short, mournful songs and called my friends on my cell phone when I knew they wouldn't be home so I could record these on their voice-mail. I didn't think about my characters, but every day I sketched the old stone wall outside my studio, noting the slightest changes in the weight and shape of the new-fallen snow.

I become obsessed with the stone walls that were scattered like broken, human music across the estate, and spent hours following their weave through the snowy woods. They were made from clearing the fields, were used to mark boundaries. They were built using large rocks, often glacial till, for the base. The size of the stones got progressively smaller as the wall got higher. All the walls were thigh height because that is as high as a man can lift a stone without strain, without having to raise his hands above his heart.

Spring never came at the arts colony. The snow continued to fall. Deer came out of the heavy snow of the woods to walk on the main road and were hit regularly by the cars that travelled the slick winter distance between our town and the next.

For a while I stopped going to dinner in the main house because the other artists were spooked that I had given up writing my novel. They were afraid it was catching. I hoarded the lunch food and for a number of days dined only on fruit and cookies and carrot sticks.

At the time I didn't know what to say about any of this. Giving up my novel was mysterious and terrifying and yet there was a freedom to it that I don't remember ever having had before. I would lie awake at nights in the studio, the snow unfurling against the window by my bed—the woods lit up like an X-ray—and I would listen to the hammering of the sculptor who was in the studio next to mine and liked to work late. The sound was rhythmical, each rise and fall of his arm like the rise and fall of my own breath. The noise filled the night, fitting it so perfectly that I couldn't imagine a better answer to the stars or the owl or the moving shadows of the deer out among the snowy trees.

On one of my last days at the colony I went to help another sculptor with her piece. I had started to lend myself out to the artists who were still engaged with their work. We were in her studio, a replicated Italian church. I was holding the sides of her sculpture together so she could close it with wire thread. The room was bright with morning as I stood there, pressing my hands against the metal in the exact position of prayer, and she passed the needle through one series of holes and out another, the wire stitches like sutures.

And in this way she mended me. In this way, I was mended.

Just because I was good at writing, and you were good at the piano, didn't mean that we were immune to the other arts. It was creativity in general that raged in us, and although we found a place to put it, a place where we could answer it best, I think that whatever our circumstances we would have found a way to express that creativity, and that was the real gift. That is what made us and kept us free.

Your first poem about the dawn was about light and movement, about the contrast between the artificial light of the hospital room and the natural light of the world outside the window. Some of the language was formal, but there were places where you sounded exactly like yourself, where your voice rang through.

I felt sorry for the dawn. It is so beautiful, / fragile, but yet badly respected by the day, you wrote.

The weather on the second morning was stormier, and you talked about the grey clouds and the turbulent sky. You wrote, *The grey and white colours are evenly dispersed. / Today we are happy with the black and white movie.*

Creativity leaves a mark. It leaves words, music, for those of us who have stayed behind after you've gone. I can listen to your CDs in my car and the essence of you is suddenly there with me as I speed along the highway towards Toronto, or meander up the country roads to my cottage.

The fact that you spent those two days at the end of September when you were in hospital writing poetry fills me with admiration for you, and with optimism. It is not that the creative urge transcends death, but it is something to shore up against it, and it keeps its meaning, right to the end, to the very last breath. Art is always about the possible, is its own form of hope.

Somewhere a door has opened and somebody has / begun their day.

32

I have been to so many of your concerts over the years, Martin, that I can no longer list or remember them. I used to have a file folder where I kept the various programs and ticket stubs, but at a certain point I gave up adding to it. Now, of course, since you've died, and since you kept everything, I have access to all of this information again.

One of the concerts I enjoyed most was at the National Physical Laboratories in England. A group of scientists had organized a lunchtime series at their workplace. They invited various musicians to come and play for them in a lecture hall cum concert hall. The acoustics were good, and I remember sitting up near the back of the rise of seats and watching the scientists in their white lab coats, quietly eating their sandwiches and listening.

Afterwards we sat outside on a bench, having a cigarette as the scientists scurried back and forth between the buildings. You must have been living in England then, and I was over for a visit. I don't remember, but it doesn't matter. There was a lot of overlap to our lives in those days. We were made of each other then.

The National Physical Laboratories don't seem to have concerts any more. Maybe they don't feel the need to continue to celebrate the connection between music and science. Maybe they are too busy doing what they do, as the U.K.'s national measurement institute, which is to apply "the most accurate measurement standards" to science and technology.

33

The river that was at the base of the valley you could see from your hospital window at the end of September was not dissimilar to the river at my cottage, although I never thought this before you were dying. But it makes sense that I chose to own a piece of land that echoed a place where we had spent time as children, where we had felt wild and free.

After you died I spent a lot of time at the cottage. I barely had any energy to move, but I could sit by the river and watch it.

The river wraps around the land, like two bodies spooning in bed or the symbols for yin and yang, one in motion, one still. When the river is low, the land seems predominant—you stand on the land

and look at the river; the land is safety, high ground, the stable, constant world. But when the river is high, the land seems fragile, about to be washed away, the fast-forward motion of the water suddenly seems dangerous, and it feels as if the land will not protect you any longer. But the river is always allied with the land that borders it. One creates the other, and the lesson of the river is to learn when to be the river, and when to be the land—when to push forward, and when to remain perfectly still.

The river makes no sound when it is fully flooded. It has filled its voice. The surface is dark, and the current moves the water forward in one long, undulating ribbon. But when the river is low, it is all noise and gurgle, rocks exposed, a small waterfall that bubbles and churns. The water rattles with its own emptiness.

Some people can stand beside a rushing river and feel restless, feel that the relentless force of the water wants to move them into action. But when I stand beside the river, I am grateful for the forward surge of the water. It allows me to remain motionless because the water is doing the moving for me.

Shortly after you were diagnosed, you came with your girlfriend to the cottage for the weekend. You sat in a chair on the grass in front of the river, but you didn't see it. You were so distracted by the fact of your cancer, and by your task that weekend of having to phone your various employers to let them know that you were terminal. These conversations were hard ones to have and so you punctuated them with walks up the road and cups of herbal tea.

The truth is that if you hadn't been about to die, you still might not have noticed the river. You were often restless and distracted. Not so much when we were young, but increasingly so as you got older and busier. It was hard for you to be where you were, except when you were working, when you were play-ing the piano.

Dying brought you back to the present, although not entirely. You were still distracted, but you were also capable of existing in the place where you were situated.

You were never again at the cottage, and I wish that day that you had been able to relinquish enough fear and control to watch the river, to let it carry your burdens away.

As children we spent a lot of time fishing. As adults, we wriggled like worms on a hook in our intimate relationships—twisting this way to please, that way to avoid telling the truth of how we really felt.

Your death has given me no choice but to slow down. This has meant that, perhaps for the first time in my life, I know what I'm feeling when I'm feeling it, that I'm able to fully experience the present moment.

This may be why the completely unexpected happened and I fell in love again. It saddens me that you'll never meet Nancy, and that my new life is so far removed from my old one. And it feels strange to me that your death is the hinge between those two worlds, the point at which everything changed.

I felt you partially leave two days before you died.
I told the nurse on duty that I thought something
was different, but she checked your stats and said
nothing had changed. Maybe nothing had changed
externally, but something had shifted in you. I
could feel that you were less present, that you were
unhooking yourself from life. Not that you were giving up, because you were someone who never gave
up or lost hope, but that you were less attached to
the moment everyone else was existing in.

When my first dog, Hazel, died a few days after
I got back from Vancouver, in the same week as
you, she approached death in a different way. She
lay awake at night, staring off into the darkness, as

though she were waiting for something, with a look in her eyes that I'd never seen before.

She waited for death. You left when you sensed it was coming.

36

In the end, you can step out of the room or you can't. The body leaks or it holds.

Your body was constantly leaking. Your blood vessels wouldn't bear up, and the smell that lifted from your skin was the smell of the drugs they were continuously pumping into you. The smell was sweet and cloying, a bit like decaying flowers.

I remember how Grandad hated lilacs because he said they were exactly what death smelled like, what dead bodies smelled like. But I found the scent of flowers on your skin a comfort. It wasn't a bad scent, and it wouldn't have bothered you if you had been able to smell it for yourself.

But you would have hated how your body looked

after the operations. There were bags to drain the incision in your belly, and bags to collect your urine and fluids, bags to drip fluids back into you. There was a PICC line in your neck, a nasty hole bored right into your jugular vein to expedite the injection of drugs. This hole was always bleeding a little and looked sore. Your whole body was swollen because your kidneys weren't functioning properly, which made you look so strange because you were also skeletal. Never anything but thin, you had dropped to under a hundred pounds with the cancer.

Most of your body was draped with a sheet, to spare anyone from seeing the gruesome incision and its attendant bags.

Your face was just a skull covered with skin. I hadn't realized that there was fat around the temples until I saw your temples caved in. There was sweat on your forehead from fever because your body was fighting the infection that came with the perforated bowel. The ventilator split your lips and made sores at the corners of your mouth. Of all of it, the venti-lator was the worst, because it prevented you from talking, from telling us what you wanted, from hav-ing a voice. At the beginning, after the first opera-tion, when we were hopeful you would recover, we were told that the ventilator would be coming out

any day, but that day just kept getting pushed back.
I wish now that we had insisted they remove it from
you, or that you had managed to tear it out, as you
tried to do before they increased your sedation.

But even if we had insisted, I'm not sure that the
medical staff would have taken you off the ventilator, that we could have made them do it. They controlled the mechanics of your body.

The hopeful scenerio was that you would beat the
infection caused by the perforated bowel and the
ventilator would be removed and you would be able
to go home. You would still die from the cancer, of
course, but later, in the spring, perhaps as late as
your birthday. It seems fair to say that this would
have happened if there hadn't been a further perfo-
ration in the bowel that they didn't catch in that first
emergency surgery. When they told me that they'd
have to operate again, I just stood at the nurses' station and cried. I knew that although you had the
strength and will to survive one major operation,
you probably wouldn't survive two.

37

In the late winter, ten months before you died, when my life was still a life I recognized, I woke early one morning in my old house and came downstairs to make coffee. That house had French doors that opened out onto the garden. I saw a movement outside and walked up to the French doors to see, on the other side of the doors, a hawk devouring a songbird.

The hawk was right up against the glass, six inches from my living room. I was able to sit down in a chair right in front of the bird and it didn't notice me there.

It was late February or early March. There was still snow on the ground, although it was constantly melting and refreezing, so the snow was uneven and hard. The hawk had the songbird pinned down in a hollow, one talon holding the body prone, while it methodically ripped the feathers from the bird with its beak.

It was a slow task, and the hawk was deliberate and focused, intent on stripping the bird and then eating it. The removal of the songbird's plumage reduced it to a generic piece of meat, and I wondered at the time if it was important for the hawk to obliterate the identity of the bird before consuming it, as though a bird that was recognizably a bird would be harder for another bird to devour.

Whatever the reason, the hawk carefully pulled all the feathers from the body of the songbird and then ripped open the chest cavity and dipped its beak inside. Holding the bird firmly with the one talon, the hawk started to pull out and eat the entrails. Blood dripped from its beak and stained its chest feathers and the snow on the ground beneath the little songbird.

Around this time, Hazel came downstairs to see what had become of me, and the hawk caught the movement of the dog through the glass and started. It grabbed the limp carcass of the songbird in its talons and lifted over the snow and the backyard, flapping up and over the fence, presumably to land in another, more private spot in which to finish eating.

Never, in my years of living in that house, and my years of living in previous houses, had anything like that happened before. It was strange on two counts—not only because it happened in a city yard, but because it happened right up against the glass of the French doors. It unnerved me, and it wasn't hard to imagine that the carnage was for my benefit, that death was coming to my house.

And, of course, it did.

You died within that year, and Hazel died, and the winter after you died was an Ontario winter you actually would have liked—not like the previous two cold and snowy winters that you had had to endure when you moved back to Toronto—but a mild, practically snowless winter that pretty much ended in February when the crocuses and snowdrops started to bloom.

After I came back from Vancouver the second time, after cleaning out your apartment, I stood in the backyard one day, calling for the new dog to come in, and I looked down and noticed that there were still the feathers of that murdered bird on the patio by my feet, that there were still spots of blood staining the flagstones.

38

The day you died there was a full moon. It was a December moon, the moon with the highest trajectory across the sky because the midwinter night is of much longer duration than the day. The sun has a low arc at this point in the year, and the moon is visible overhead for a greater length of time.

After you died we walked out into the cold of the parking lot. The sun was setting red behind the mountains, and the moon had already risen. We drove, with your friends, to the pub where you used to go for a beer, and being in different cars, some of us got lost on the way and we all arrived at different times.

The pub was called the Mountain Shadow Inn, and it had the look of a Swiss chalet, lots of carved wood inside, a balcony on the outside that hung over the entranceway. The eaves were decorated with gingerbread trim, some of it painted red and white. The building sat by itself on a patch of land just off the highway. There was nothing else around, no other buildings. The moonlight made the grass look silver as we walked across it.

Upstairs, where you used to like to go, there was a large-screen TV overtop of a fireplace, and lots of nooks and crannies to sit in.

We waited for you, all of us, and we turned towards every person who came up the staircase, full of anticipation. Because it was like you to be the last to arrive, overbooked and hurrying from one assignation to another, your briefcase stuffed with music and overflowing, your long legs practically running because you knew you were late and didn't want to be.

We waited for you, because it was still too soon to break this habit, to fully accept that you had died, that we had left your body behind in the hospital, that we were doing something you liked without you.

All the moons in a year have names. October is the harvest moon. May is the planting moon. January is the wolf moon. The December moon is known, across most cultures, as the cold moon, or the long night moon.

39

I'm in the West again, in Banff, on my way to Vancouver. I'm on a book tour and today is a layover day. I'm at the arts centre, a place where I've been before, both as a resident and to teach. It's a place I always encouraged you to visit, but you never were able to organize a break from your busy working life.

You would love it here, Martin. The mountains are all around, ringing the town, so that wherever you look there is bare rock and trees, sheer cliffs, and snow on the summits. The mountains are jagged lines against the sky and look particularly spectacular at dusk.

There's a small mountain by the arts centre, a big

hill really, but nice to wander up. Usually when I'm here I walk up it every day, but right now there are three cougars living on it and it isn't safe. There's also been a grizzly spotted down by the river near town, so it's not possible to walk there either. Apparently last week one of the cougars ate an elk on the lawn in front of the dining hall.

You always attached yourself romantically to anywhere you travelled, and came home wanting to move there. You travelled widely, but you only ever lived in three places—Toronto, Vancouver, and England. For all the opportunity you had to live abroad—an EU passport, the fact that music is its own language and you could have found work anywhere you went—you were never able to fulfill your dreams of living in Paris, or Prague, or Vienna.

I think we both thought of the place we had come from, Scarborough, as a place to leave. I moved there with Mum and Dad, straight off the boat from England, into a newly built suburban split-level on an unfenced, lawnless lot. Our parents put down grass, planted trees, made gardens. They planted a tree for each of us, although mine had to be pulled down quite early on as it had been positioned too close to the house and the roots had crawled under the foundation and interfered with the sewage system. Your tree is still there though, a huge red maple standing sentinel in the northwest corner of the backyard.

When we were growing up, the rural bones of the place still showed through. There were fields and ponds, an old barn down the road, an inn from the 1800s up the road. The William Wallace Inn was a dilapidated brick house by the time we arrived and was used for various strange business enterprises. There was always a German shepherd on guard and barking hoarsely from an upstairs window.

Once the inn was a Plexiglas factory and we could go up there at night and collect bits of the discarded Plexiglas from the big piles of sawdust out back. Before the building was an inn it was undoubtedly a family home for wealthy people and they would have owned the surrounding land, which included the land our suburban house had been built on.

An old pear tree stood outside the big brick inn, and for years after the house had been pulled down, I would collect pears from this tree on my way home from school. The tree was eventually torn down to make way for a new housing development.

But this was the landscape of our childhood, these bits of the old countryside—ancient fruit trees, ponds and streams, thickets of sumac, and fields of long grass. The people in the houses on our street used to dump their leaves and grass clippings at the edge of one of these fields, and periodically one boy or another would set them on fire.

We dug holes in this field to shelter in. For years we trod a path through it on the mile walk downhill to school. I remember the rabbit warrens in the banks, the worn dirt of the ground, smooth and slick in places as the leather in an old saddle.

We were always a mile from school, always the farthest away from both primary and secondary institutions. We walked together to school when we were young, sometimes trudging four miles a day if we were coming home for lunch. You started this walk earlier than me, because I was older and expected to look after you on the journey. You were probably walking that four miles from the age of six.

Across from the road to our primary school was a curving downhill trail called the cinder path, which led between the houses to the streets of the village that unwound a level below our suburban streets. This community was also a suburb, but had the name of a village. Our parents, having come from English villages, thought that because the suburb was called Guildwood Village it would resemble the villages they had known, and this made them decide to live there.

The cinder path led down to streets that, in turn, led to a park on the edge of the bluffs overlooking Lake Ontario, the feature that defined our particular patch of the world. The park is one of the few things in our old neighbourhood that is as it ever was, with its small copses of sumac trees and open meadow before the sheer three-hundred-foot drop to the beach below. The boiler of a sunken ship used to be visible from the top of the cliffs. Swimming out to it was a popular thing to do when we were teenagers.

The park was always a place to party. I remember being there one night with a group of older kids, when I was about fifteen, and seeing juddering lights moving through the darkness towards us, realizing, too late, that it was a police car driving over the bumpy ground of the field.

The bluffs are still spectacular. It's exciting to stand as close to the edge as possible. Being up so high means that you look down on the seam where the water meets the sky, not across to it, and the two appear to be one fabric, as if there is no divide between lake and sky.

The moon looks amazing when seen from the top

of the bluffs, and it's hard not to believe that this was the place you imagined when you were writing your musical, when you were planning the lovers' duet taking place on a clifftop.

You and I went to the bluffs many times. I remember walking there with you once late at night, in the middle of the night, and we sat on the curb in front of the park entrance, smoking cigarettes and talking about our parents. We used to look back at our childhood as a mystery that needed to be solved, when really it was just that we were no longer children, that our childhood selves were unrecognizable to the people we had become.

I remember the brands of the cigarettes we smoked—Player's Light for you, Craven "A" for me (because I liked the word *craven*). I remember that you sat on my right on the curb, as later you sat on my right at the performance of *South Pacific* in New York. I remember we were wearing jeans and T-shirts, that the night was warm and expansive, that there were no sounds except for our voices, that the sky was full of stars, and that we looked at the stars often, heads tilted back, or lying down on our backs in the grass.

You walked down to that park when you were staying with Mum and Dad during the course of chemo. You had bought yourself a cap to wear in case you lost your hair (although you never did lose your hair) and one of your friends took a picture of you, standing on the edge of the bluffs, wearing that cap. Your face is skeletal in the photo, and when Mum wanted to include it in your memorial slideshow, I told her not to because it didn't look like you. But really, it did look like you. It just looked like you dying.

I never thought we came from anywhere because the landscape we lived in as children changed all the time. Houses were built in the fields. Anything old was demolished. Ponds were filled in. Trees were chopped down. Most of the landmarks from our childhood have completely disappeared.

But now I see that where we came from is the space, not the individual objects. We came from the sprawl of the suburbs, where each back garden was half an acre and each driveway was big enough for a full game of street hockey. We came from the long horizon of lake, and the dark summer sky, full of stars. We came from wide streets, from fields with grasses arcing taller than our heads, from creeks that frothed and raced after a spring rain, from the train trestles we used to run across, from all the trees we used to climb.

And that is what we carried with us into adulthood, this desire for space, for the empty horizon. When you drove across Canada, from Vancouver to Toronto, you took photos of the journey. Most of those photos are of the landscape—fields and lakes, open sky, train tracks, the long stretch of highway in front of your car. I know what the long view felt like to you, because it feels the same way to me. It feels like freedom. It feels like coming home.

In Vancouver, I go to your old apartment out in Burnaby. It's a long and arduous journey by bus, and I get off in the wrong place and have to walk the steep part of the hill that I was trying to avoid.

There's a FOR RENT sign on the front railing of the building, but a barbecue on your balcony, so it's not your apartment that's vacant. The cedar and bushes in front of the building have grown fast in the year and a half since I was last here. Another year and your balcony will be entirely screened in green, an oasis protected from the busy street. I can picture you walking out into a lush cave of vegetation to sit and have a break from practising. I can imagine your living room shimmering green in the sunlight.

I feel like I should say something to you at the apartment, but, as at the cemetery, that just seems stupid, so I don't. I take a photo for Cathy and walk back down the hill, stopping every now and then to look south over the view of Vancouver that you liked so much. In the other direction, the line of mountains is obscured by clouds today, and I can't see any part of them at all.

Cathy suggested going to have a coffee in your honour at the café down the street from your apartment, but I feel too miserable to do that, so I just get back on the bus and return to the hotel.

It's hard to be in Vancouver. I go past places where you used to work, one right by where I'm staying, and this morning when I was on my way to the bus stop, there was piano music spilling out of an open upstairs window. That was, in fact, the last place you worked, and you were there that night, a few hours before you went into hospital. The very last time you played the piano was in that building.

I look for you in the places where you were, and of course, you're not there. It's no comfort to go to your apartment, but I go anyway. It's not like I need to be reminded of you, like I don't think of you all the time anyway. But it turns out that parts of the journey are so much about you that it does make me feel I was meant to ride that bus back to your apartment. The classical record shop on West Hastings with all the old piano recordings in the window, much of it music you have played. The sign on another building across the street that said, WHAT WAS ONCE, ALWAYS HAS BEEN, SOMEHOW NEVER AGAIN. The old stuffed koala bear in the junk shop that looked just like the stuffed koala you used to have when you were a little boy—when you slept in bed with all your stuffed animals, your favourites being two monkeys you named Jiffy and Jocko, who slept on either side of you, like guards.

I walk all the way down the hill and halfway up the next hill on my way home, and when I finally stop to catch the bus, I am standing directly opposite the funeral home where your body was taken after you died.

What I really hate about you being dead is that you're not in your apartment, that you don't come to the door when I ring the buzzer, that you don't come out with me onto the streets of Burnaby, down to the coffee shop, that you don't say, *Let's stop and have a coffee,* that you aren't with me on the bus (because that bus was the one that took you directly to work), and that I'm not waiting for you to finish work right now, listening to the sound of your piano fall from the open window above this street, that it's just me doing these things in your name, that they feel useless, that you're not there to sanction my activities, or argue with them. You're not there to stop them from being necessary.

41

I'm back in Kingston again. For the first time, when I stepped through the door the new house felt like home, like somewhere I belonged. I find that I want to stay in this house. I don't want to move, to keep moving, the way I have for all of my adult life. I want to stay here and fix this place up, spend money on it when I have some money to spend.

It was sunny today and I took the dogs out to the fields. They ran through the grass, splashed across the muddy river, rolled in something dead. I yelled at them and they paid no attention. On leash, returning to the car, they practically yanked my arms out of their sockets.

It's good to be home.

My hair has grown longer during my travels. It got tangled today by the wind and the walk. On the way back to the house, I caught a glimpse of myself in the rear-view mirror. My windblown hair, dark and curly, looked exactly like your hair, Martin. There was a full moment where I didn't know if it was you I saw in the car mirror, or me.

When the dogs are together sometimes they pee at exactly the same second, or react identically to an outside interest or threat. They are so alike in those moments that it is as though they share the same brain. Maybe that is what it is to be siblings, the similarities are buried so deep in the cells that they aren't questioned or acknowledged—they just are.

The first thing I want to do to my house is to level the crooked floors, to shore up the beams in the basement, and to bring the timbers of the building back into alignment. I want the structure of the house to be as it was when it was built.

42

We each remember you most clearly from when you most belonged to us. Mum thinks of you when you were a baby and little boy. I remember you when we were both teenagers and young adults. Cathy recalls the time you came home to live for a while and you and she were the only children in the house. Your old girlfriends think of when they were together with you. Death makes you ours again, even if it's only in memory.

This is what we're left with—memory, your music, and the physical objects that remain from your life.

I finally open one of the boxes I brought back from your Vancouver apartment, the one with the items that were beside your bed.

There are several books. There is my novel, with a 7-Eleven phone card as the bookmark on page 54. There are two books about New York that you bought when we were there together on that last trip. I'm sure you hadn't started either, but meant to read both. One is a historical atlas of the city, and the other is a collection of photographs, portraits of men and women who work in vanishing professions—mannequin maker, television repairman among them. The explanation of each job is on the facing page to the photograph.

The last book is a Russian science-fiction story that is also a political allegory about Stalin's dictatorship. *The Fatal Eggs* is the tale of a scientist whose experiments go wrong and, instead of creating a utopian world, he creates a nightmare scenario of plagues and violence. You had only got to page 10 in this book, but I know you were enjoying it because I remember you talking about it.

On page 10, the professor is just starting his experiments. Nothing is out of control yet.

The piece of paper that you used to mark where you were in the book is a map to one of the dance schools you played at. On the back of it you have written a list of things to do: *RAD money, invoice school board, Mum, call real estate agent, bills.* I'm always trying to decide if these lists you made, of which there were many, were written before you knew you were dying, or afterwards. I don't know why this is important, but it is. And this list, I think, judging by the note to call the real estate agent, was written just before you were diagnosed, when you were trying to sell your house in Toronto in order to move back to the West, before you gave up on that idea and rented your house out instead.

Your lists are often written in light pencil and are maddeningly hard to read. But these were lists meant only for you, and you wouldn't care that they're hard to read or incomplete. On one loose sheet of paper are the barely legible thoughts: *Maybe people aren't sometimes lonely, so much as alone,* and, *Whether or not it is entirely accurate, it is better to think good of things, people, the world etc.*

Some of the items that were beside your bed have already been dispensed with—the pile of loose change, your cell phone and charger, the puddle of clothes that you had stepped out of at the end of your last real day on earth. You were in such pain when the ambulance came that you couldn't even put your pants on. You just went to hospital in what you were sleeping in—a T-shirt and underwear, with a long coat thrown overtop for decency's sake.

The box also contains things that I took from your apartment. There are CDs from your collection, programs from your recitals. There are two beer coasters with the words *Marty's Bar* on them, which someone must have given you. There's the obituary, carefully cut out of the newspaper, for your elementary school classmate who died at the age of thirty-eight from a heart problem he didn't know he had—the first of your peers to die. And there are various pieces of your identification that I couldn't part with, either because they had photos of you (your work identity badges, a transit pass), or because they were from an earlier, sweeter time (your university student card, your Surrey County library card from when you lived in England). The photo on the transit pass shows you with a full beard. The photo on your work identity badge from the last day of work that you did has you in the red T-shirt that I wear all the time now because it still smells, faintly, of you. In that photo you look gaunt. In that photo you are just weeks away from being dead.

After you died, I flew home to Kingston. We buried you, Christmas came and went, uncelebrated, and then I gathered my strength and went back to the coast in January to clear out your apartment.

I took the train instead of flying because I wanted to feel every inch of the countryside that had existed between us all those years we lived in different places; because I didn't really want to arrive, didn't want to have to face your life without you in it; because you had driven across the country when you journeyed from Vancouver to Toronto, and I wanted to see what you had seen. It was winter, so I couldn't make the drive myself. The conditions would have been too dangerous, too unpredictable. But from the train window—seeing the snow, the sky, the trees, the endless prairie—I felt the distance, watched the countryside open and close. The slowness and deliberateness of the journey felt like the only way to move towards the task I was dreading.

And now it's over, all of it. You are a body in the cold ground, a handful of identity cards, the books you were reading, the CDs you played, the clothes you wore, the lists you made, the concerts you gave, the places you went, and what you brought back to remind yourself you'd been there.

43

One of the pieces you had planned to play if you had lived long enough was John Cage's *4' 33."* This tribute to silence, to listening, was something you'd performed before, years ago. I was at that first performance, and I remember the nervous laughter from the audience as you sat down at the piano, hands folded together in your lap, back straight, and didn't play a note. That laughter subsided into an uncomfortable silence, and that awkward self-consciousness was followed by a growing attentiveness, all in the space of five minutes.

When we were young we talked about what we wanted to be, how we were going to serve our particular art forms, what we wanted to achieve within

them. In the middle of life, having largely succeeded
at what we had set out to do, we realized the limitations of our particular choices, and indeed of the arts
to which we had chosen to devote our lives. I wish
that we had been able to have more conversations
about what we learned from those limitations.

The problem with writing, for me, is that it fol-
lows experience. It doesn't recreate it, but rather lags
behind. Writing done well makes a new thing of the
experience it's trying to describe, but it's not always
possible to do it well and so the execution of it is
often unsatisfactory, although the ideas and sensa-
tions behind the execution never are. Virginia Woolf
described writing as stumbling after your own voice.
I wish she'd gone on to say that rarely, if ever, do
you catch up to it. Increasingly I would rather live
a perfect day than write about one, but when I was
younger this desire was exactly opposite.

Music is always imposing itself. It's aggressive.
It takes a space and fills it with sound. It colonizes
silence. I can see that the effort it takes to do this,
the confidence needed to continually make this asser-
tion, could easily fail. Is the noise of music really better than the silence it is invading? This will always be
the question. I can understand why you said that you
thought John Cage's music of silence, in three move-

ments, each signalled by the opening and closing of the piano lid, was the greatest piece of music ever composed. I can understand why you would want to return to it when you were dying.

The piece is deceptively simple. In the original 1961 score there is no proportional notation. The three movements are indicated solely by roman numerals, followed by the word TACET in capital letters after each one. *Tacet* is the word used for an orchestral part to indicate that a particular instrument does not play during a movement. It is not standard practice to have this apply to a solo composition. But although performed originally on piano, Cage's piece has subsequently been performed by other instruments, and by full orchestras, so the orchestral instruction for silence—*tacet*—makes more sense than any other word used in its place.

About the writing of his piece, Cage said: "Composing's one thing, performing's another, listening's a third. What can they have to do with one another?" He liked to think of his composition as not needing a performer, that it was essentially a vehicle for listening. And about listening he went on to state that "What we hear is determined by our own emptiness, our own receptivity; we receive to the extent we are empty to do so."

At some point while writing to you, I thought that I should mirror the structure of Cage's piece. I wanted to format my thoughts according to the form of *4' 33"*—which, after careful timing, I determined was approximately three and a half pages of written text. Each section in this book was to have been three and a half pages long. Each section was to have been your playing of Cage's piece, and what I was hearing while you were sitting motionless at the piano. Death has made you this performer for eternity now.

But my grief is not that orderly, or that disciplined. It lopes ahead, stops short. I am not really able to contain it, merely follow where it leads. My only structural constraint is that I have decided on forty-five segments for this piece, one for every year you were alive.

But this act of writing is indeed an act of listening, and it is as though you are on stage, at the piano, in your tails, with the light behind you, and I am sitting in the audience, listening to the thoughts in my head, to the scuff of feet on the wooden floor, to the birdsong outside the window, the crackle as a cough drop is unwrapped. I am sitting here, waiting for you to make a sound, to guide me through this moment, when, in fact, the truth of this moment is that you are giving it to me, in its entirety.

44

The worst day was the last day. This was the day when you died, but it was also the day when you opened your eyes. The night before, the doctor had talked to us about taking you off life support because you weren't going to recover. Your liver, already compromised by the cancer, couldn't handle the drugs being pumped into your body to keep you alive, and it had begun to shut down. One of the side effects of a malfunctioning liver is brain damage, and we were told that you were probably already suffering impairment.

When you gave me power of attorney, I asked you what measures you wanted me to take in case you couldn't make a decision for yourself. *Never say die,*

you said, which at the time made us laugh, but at the
end was a hard wish to interpret. I knew you would
not want to give up if there was the faintest hope
that something could be done. But in this case,
when you were being kept alive by machines, and
when this would go on for a few days more, a week
perhaps, what did you want me to do? Was the fact
of being alive, even with the needles in your body,
and the tube down your throat, and the miasma of
drugs swimming through your veins, worth it? Were
we being gently persuaded by the medical person-
nel to end your life because they saw no future to
it, and because they needed the ICU bed? Was the
hope they offered at the beginning and the defeat-
ism they conceded to at the end simply part of a
script they used with terminal ICU patients?

In the early days of your hospital stay, after the
first operation, when the spirit was one of optimism and the doctors were talking of your being
able to recover from the surgery and return home
for your last few months, there was discussion of
your permanently wearing a colostomy bag, having limited mobility, needing a hospital bed in
the apartment, and needing care. None of these
things would have broken you. I know you would
have been depressed by the physical limitations,

but you would have continued to live your life because you were a fighter, and because you loved being alive. You were inherently optimistic, and that optimism would have resurfaced after a brief period where you adapted to your new and challenging circumstances.

But now we feared you had suffered brain damage. If you were yourself and dealing with infirmity, that was one thing, but if your brain was impaired, you wouldn't be yourself, and this, I'm sure, would have caused you extreme distress and would have been impossible to reconcile.

When your eyes were closed, as they had been since the second operation, and the machines confirmed the drop in your blood pressure and the acceleration of your heart rate, and I could smell the drugs leaking from your skin, it was not hard to believe that your brain function was affected.

But that last day, you opened your eyes and you looked around. Your face remained impassive, as impassive as it could remain with the ventilator taped across your mouth, forcing it into an unnatural and open position.

When I sat beside your bed, you looked at me, and we stared into each other's eyes. You rarely broke the contact, but if a nurse came into the room, you followed her with your eyes until she left again, and then you returned your gaze to me. The entire time I was looking at you, I was willing you to communicate what you wanted me to do for you. Were you ready to die, or did you want to live another day, another handful of days? Was there any pleasure to be had from the sun at the window, or from our faces, or from your own thoughts?

Once, long ago, we were in our parents' house and you were talking about an experience you'd had. It was dinner and we were all sitting around the kitchen table as you recounted this event that, halfway through your telling of it, I realized was actually something that had happened to me.

"Hey," I said, "that's my memory. Not yours."

I went on to fill in the details, but it took some convincing before you would give up ownership of the memory, and even then, you did so reluctantly.

Because what happened to me could just as easily have happened to you. At one time in our lives, perhaps all through our lives, our experiences and our reactions to them could have been interchangeable. Love and shared interests, time spent together, these were things that were layered on top of our fundamental sameness, a similarity that was bred in the bone. Undeniable, and unshakeable.

I should have known what you wanted—you of all people—because we'd been children together, and adults together, because in some inescapable way we knew each other better than anyone else. I still keep your secrets, for God's sake, even now, when there's no real need to keep them.

But I didn't know what you wanted me to do for you. Marty, I didn't have a fucking clue.

Your eyes were such a beautiful dark brown, the same shade as your hair. I could tell that you were looking to me for information, but I wasn't sure what information you needed. I don't know if you wanted me to tell you that you were minutes away from dying, but, rightly or wrongly, I didn't do this.

Mostly I just held your gaze, without tears or words. I held your gaze, and then we shut you down.

45

On one of the days shortly after you were diagnosed, when I came to the house to take you to chemo, you were playing the piano. I walked up the stairs from the front door and into the living room. You were sitting at the piano, your piano, which Mum and Dad had moved into their house. The living room was nothing but baby grand pianos, yours blocking off the entrance to the dining room and Mum's by the window. Between the pianos was a small oasis of chairs and a coffee table on a patch of carpet.

It was a sunny afternoon in early fall. I remember the sun coming through the window and falling on the objects in the room, how strong the light was, and how I turned to it as you were playing because I thought I might cry. You were playing so confidently, as confidently as you'd always played. Your playing is the most familiar sound of my life. I thought, standing there in the living room of the house we grew up in, that this sound, your sound, would be finite, that there wouldn't be many more times I would hear you play.

So, I desperately tried to hang onto that moment. I tried to absorb your playing into my consciousness, into my body, but your notes disappeared the instant they hit the air.

Music comes undone. It unravels into silence.

You were playing the Debussy, the *Suite bergamasque*.

It's beautiful, isn't it, you said, looking up from the piano.

"It's really beautiful," I said.

What I remember now from that day is not the music, but the silence that followed the music, the slant of light at the window, the rustle of paper when I said, "We have to go now," and you closed your music decisively and stood up from the bench and put on your jacket and we walked out into the sunshine.

Acknowledgements

I would like to thank my agent, Clare Alexander, for her care and guidance during the writing of this book.

I would like to thank my editor at Serpent's Tail, Rebecca Gray, for her support, understanding, and encouragement.

Sections from this book have been previously published in *The Queen's Quarterly*, *The Walrus*, and the *Independent* in the UK.

The score of John Cage's 4'33" is Copyright © 1960 by Henmar Press, Inc. Used by permission of C.F. Peters Corporation. All rights reserved.

The quotes from John Cage are from *No Such Thing as Silence: John Cage's 4'33"* by Kyle Gann, published by Yale University Press.

Grief is a solitary experience, but I was not alone on my journey and I would like to thank the family and friends who accompanied me, supported me, and made life possible during my brother's illness and death: Mary Louise Adams, Tama Baldwin, Andrea Bergamini, Elizabeth Christie, Nancy Jo Cullen, Sue Goyette, Cathy Humphreys, Frances Humphreys, Anthony Humphreys, Michelle Jaffe, Walter Lloyd, Eleanor MacDonald, Daintry Norman, Joanne Page, Anne Peters, Su Rynard. Not to mention the vizsla sisters, Charlotte and Violet.

Thanks as well to Mary Ordanis and Sue Worrall for their assistance to Martin during his move.

I would also like to thank my brother's friends for their compassion, kindness and support during his last months. Martin once said, *I have the best friends.* And he did.

Peter Canakis, Cheryl Carruthers, Jessica Chang, Alan Crane, Melissa Duchak, Bernie Duerksen, Holly Duff, Phil Duncan, Isaac Juarez Flores, James Langevin, Charlie Ringus, Tom Saunders, Ward and Jill Smith, Sherman Stave, Cam Walker, Tanis Wilkie.